Edward Bond

LEAR

WITHDRAWN

EYRE METHUEN LTD
11 NEW FETTER LANE LONDON EC4

First published 1972 by Eyre Methuen
11 New Fetter Lane London EC4P 4EE
© 1972 by Edward Bond
Reprinted 1973 and 1976
Printed Offset Litho in Great Britain by
Cox & Wyman Ltd, Fakenham, Norfolk

ISBN 0 413 28760 2 (Hardback)
ISBN 0 413 28770 x (Paperback)

Lear

Lear was first performed at the Royal Court Theatre in September 1971. Taking as its starting point the story of an autocratic monarch deposed by his two power-hungry daughters, the play presents a parable of the ruthless cruelty imposed on us by the assumptions of modern society. Lear, his daughters and their con-querors too, have all suffered and are shown suffering hideously, caught in the trap. But freed at last from his sufferings, Lear perceives and gives voice to the urgent need both for an awareness of man's trapped state and for pity as a corrective.

'He has not cultivated a garden but created a land-scape . . . it is one of the most powerful plays to have emerged in years . . . Although its tragic scale is unimaginable except in the theatre, it is not primarily a play for "theatregoers", but is meant for anyone con-cerned with our apparently hell-bent course towards self-destruction.'

Helen Dawson in *The Observer*

The photograph on the front of the cover shows Harry Andrews as Lear and Mark McManus as the Grave-digger's Boy in the Royal Court production and is reproduced by courtesy of John Haynes.

by the same author

SAVED
NARROW ROAD TO THE DEEP NORTH
EARLY MORNING
THE POPE'S WEDDING
THE SEA
BINGO

Author's Preface

I write about violence as naturally as Jane Austen wrote about manners. Violence shapes and obsesses our society, and if we do not stop being violent we have no future. People who do not want writers to write about violence want to stop them writing about us and our time. It would be immoral not to write about violence.

*

Many animals are able to be violent, but in non-human species the violence is finally controlled so that it does not threaten the species' existence. Then why is the existence of our species threatened by its violence?

I must begin with an important distinction. The predator hunting its prey is violent but not aggressive in the human way. It wants to eat, not destroy, and its violence is dangerous to the prey but not to the predator. Animals only become aggressive – that is destructive in the human sense – when their lives, territory or status in their group are threatened, or when they mate or are preparing to mate. Even then the aggression is controlled. Fighting is usually ritualized, and the weaker or badly-placed animal will be left alone when it runs away or formally submits. Men use much of their energy and skill to make more efficient weapons to destroy each other, but animals have often evolved in ways to ensure they *can't* destroy each other.

A lot has been written on this subject and it is not my job to repeat the evidence; but it shows clearly, I think, that in normal surroundings and conditions members of the same species are not dangerous to one another, but that when they are kept in adverse conditions, and forced to behave unnaturally, their behaviour deteriorates. This has been seen in zoos and laboratories. Then they become destructive and neurotic and make bad parents. They begin to behave like us.

That is all there is to our 'innate' aggression, or our 'original' sin as it was first called. There is no evidence of an aggressive *need*, as there is of sexual and feeding *needs*. We respond aggressively when we are constantly deprived of our physical and emotional needs, or when we are threatened with this; and if we are constantly deprived and threatened in this way – as human beings now are – we live in a constant state of aggression. It does not matter how much a man doing routine work in, say, a factory or office is paid: he will still be deprived in this sense. Because he is behaving in a way for which he is not designed, he is alienated from his natural self, and this will have physical and emotional consequences for him. He becomes nervous and tense and he begins to look for threats everywhere. This makes him belligerent and provocative; he becomes a threat to other people, and so his situation rapidly deteriorates.

This is all the facts justify us in concluding: aggression is an ability but not a necessity. The facts are often *interpreted* more pessimistically, but that is another matter.

If we *were* innately aggressive, in the sense that it was *necessary* for us to act aggressively from time to time, we would be condemned to live with an incurable disease; and as the suffering caused by aggression in a technological culture is so terrible, the question would arise: does the human race have any moral justification for its existence? A character in my play *Early Morning* answered no, and he tried to kill himself. It is astonishing that many people who share his beliefs are not forced to draw his conclusions, but can still go about their daily business. This ability shows mental shallowness and emotional glibness, not stoicism and spiritual strength. Their 'realism' is really only the fascism of lazy men.

Then why do we behave worse to one another than other animals? We live in ways for which we are not designed and so our daily existence interferes with our natural functioning, and this activates our natural response to threat: aggression. How has this happened? Why, in the first place, do we live in urban, crowded regimented groups, working like machines (mostly for the benefit of other men) and with no real control of our lives? Probably this situation could not have been avoided. Men did not suddenly become possessors of human minds and then use them to solve the problems of existence. These problems were constantly posed and solved within an inherited organization or social structure, and this structure was redeveloped to deal with new problems as they arose. So there was probably never much chance for new thinking. As men's minds clarified they were already living in herds or groups, and these would have evolved into tribes and societies. Like waking sleepers they would not know dream from reality.

What problems did these half-awake, superstitious men have to face? They were biologically so successful that they probably became too numerous for their environments and they could not go on living as loose bands of scavengers and hunters. And the environment itself changed, sometimes suddenly and sometimes gradually but inevitably. And perhaps the relationship between earlier instincts and human awareness produced its own problems. All these changes required adaptations in social organization and created new opportunities for leadership. Habits and techniques of control would be strengthened. In critical times any non-conformity would be a danger to the group. People who are controlled by others in this way soon lose the ability to act for themselves, even if their leaders do not make it dangerous for them to do so. And then, as I shall explain, the natural feelings of opposition become moralized and work to perpetuate the very organization they basically oppose. The whole structure becomes held together by the negative biological response to deprivation and threat – it is an organization held together by the aggression it creates. Aggression has become moralized, and morality has become a form of violence. I shall describe how this happens.

Once the social structure exists it tends to be perpetuated. The organizing groups, the leaders, receive privileges. Some of these were perhaps necessary in the critical situations that created the need for leadership. But the justification for them becomes less when they are inherited by their children. At the same time they become more extensive and entrenched. They become an injustice. But the organizing group becomes self-justifying, because although its position is unjust it is the administrator of justice. At first opposition to it will not be revolutionary or even political; it will be 'meaningless' and involve personal discontents and frustrations. When personal problems become private problems, as they must for the people involved in them, they are distorted, and then people seem to be acting in arbitrary, self-regarding ways. This can always be shown to be socially disruptive, of course. In this way an unjust society causes and defines crime; and an aggressive social structure which is unjust and must create aggressive social disruption, receives the moral sanction of being 'law and order'. Law and order is one of the steps taken to maintain injustice.

People with unjust social privileges have an obvious emotional interest in social morality. It allows them to maintain their privileges and justifies them in taking steps to do so. It reflects their fear of an opposition that would often take away everything they have, even their lives. This is one way in which social morality becomes angry and aggressive.

But there is another way. Social morality is also a safe form of obedience for many of the victims of the unjust organization. It gives them a form of innocence founded on fear – but it is never a peaceful innocence. It is a sort of character easily developed in childhood, when power relations are at their starkest. Then it is dangerous to have aggressive ideas against those in power because they can easily punish you, they are stronger and cleverer, and if you destroyed them how could you live? (In adults this becomes: We can't have a revolution because the buses wouldn't run and I'd be late for work. Or: Hitler made the trains run on time.) Our society has the structure of a pyramid of aggression and as the child is the weakest member it is at the bottom. We still *think* we treat children with special kindness and make special allowances for them, as indeed most animals do. But do we? Don't most people believe they have a right, even a duty, to use crude force against children as part of their education? Almost all organizations dealing with children are obsessed with discipline. Whenever possible we put them into uniforms and examine their minds like warders frisking prisoners. We force them to live by the clock before they can read it, though this makes no biological sense. We build homes without proper places for them. They interfere with the getting of money so mothers leave them and go to work – and some of them are no longer even physically able to feed their own children. Parents are worn out by daily competitive striving so they can't tolerate the child's natural noise and mess. They don't know why it cries, they don't know *any* of its inarticulate language. The child's first word isn't 'mummy' or 'daddy', it is 'me'. It has been learning to say it through millions of years of evolution, and it has a biological right to its egocentricity because that is the only way our species can continue.

The point is this: every child is born with certain biological expectations, or if you like species' assumptions – that it's unpreparedness will be cared for, that it will be given not only food but emotional reassurance, that its vulnerability will be shielded, that it will be born into a world waiting to receive it, and that knows *how* to receive it. But the weight of aggression in our society is so heavy that the unthinkable happens: we batter it. And when the violence is not so crude it is still there, spread thinly over years; the final effect is the same and so the dramatic metaphor I used to describe it was the stoning of a baby in its pram. This is not done by thugs but by people who like plays condemning thugs.

One way or the other the child soon learns that it is born into a strange world and not the world it evolved for: we are no longer born free. So the small, infinitely vulnerable child panics – as any animal must. It does not get the reassurance it needs, and in its fear it identifies with the people who have power over it. That is, it accepts their view of the situation, their judgement of who is right and wrong – their *morality*. But this morality – which is social morality – now has all the force of the fear and panic that created it. Morality stops being something people want and becomes what they are terrified to be without. So social morality is a form of corrupted innocence, and it is against the basic wishes of those who have been moralized in this way. It is a threat, a weapon used against their most fundamental desire for justice, without which they are not able to be happy or allow others to be happy. The aggressive response of such people has been smothered by social morality, but this only increases its tension. So they try to relieve it in extravert ways. Often they become missionaries and campaigners. They are obsessed with a need for censorship – which is only the moral justification of the peeping Tom. They find the wicked and ungodly everywhere – because these things are in themselves. Their social morality denies their need for justice, but that need is so basic it can only be escaped by dying or going mad; otherwise it must be struggled against obsessively. In this struggle pleasure becomes guilt, and the moralizing, censorious, inhuman puritans are formed. Sometimes their aggression is hidden under strenuous gleefulness, but it is surprising how little glee is reflected in their opinions and beliefs, and how intolerant, destructive and angry these guardians of morality can be.

Their morality is angry because they are in conflict with themselves. Not merely divided, but *fighting* their own repressed need for justice with all the fear and hysteria of their original panic. Because this isn't something that is done once, in childhood or later; to go on living these people must murder themselves every day. Social morality is a form of suicide. Socially moralized people must act contemptuously and angrily to all liberalism, contentment and sexual freedom, because these are the things they are fighting in themselves. There is no way out for them – it is as if an animal was locked in a cage and then fed with the key. It shakes the bars but can never get out. So other people's happiness becomes their pain, and other people's freedom reminds them of their slavery. It is as if they had created in themselves a desolate, inhospitable landscape in which they had to live out their emotional and spiritual lives. This landscape reflects, of course, the inhospitable, unjust world in which they first suffered; and it exacerbates and reinforces their aggression and seems to give it added depths of bitterness. By calling the unjust world good they recreate it in themselves and are condemned to live in it. They have not learned that when you are frightened of the dark you do not make it go away by shutting your eyes. These people are the angry, gleeful ghosts of my play, *Early Morning*.

Not all children grow up in this way, of course. Some solve the problem by becoming cynical and indifferent, others hide in a listless, passive conformity, others become criminal and openly destructive. Whatever happens, most of them will grow up to act in ways that are ugly, deceitful and violent; and the conforming, socially moralized, good citizens will be the most violent of all, because their aggression is expressed through all the technology and power of massed society. The institutions of morality and order are always more destructive than crime. This century has made that very clear.

Even if a child escapes undamaged it will still face the same problems as a man. We treat men as children. They have no real political or economic control of their lives, and this makes them afraid of society and their own impotence in it. Marx has described adult alienation very well, but we can now understand more about it. We can see that most men are spending their lives doing things for which they are not biologically designed. We are not designed for our production lines, housing blocks, even cars; and these things are not designed for us. They are designed, basically, to make profit. And because we do not even need most of the things we waste our lives in producing, we have to be surrounded by commercial propaganda to make us buy them. This life is so unnatural for us that, for straightforward biological reasons, we become tense, nervous and aggressive, and these characteristics are fed back into our young. Tension and aggression are even becoming the markings of our species. Many people's faces are set in patterns of alarm, coldness or threat; and they move jerkily and awkwardly, not with the simplicity of free animals. These expressions are signs of moral disease, but we are taught to admire them. They are used in commercial propaganda and in iconographic pictures of politicians and leaders, even writers; and of course they are taken as signs of good manners in the young.

It is for these reasons I say that society is held together by the aggression it creates, and men are not dangerously aggressive but our sort of society is. It creates aggression in these ways: first, it is basically unjust, and second it makes people live unnatural lives – both things which create a natural, biological aggressive response in the members of society. Society's formal answer to this is socialized morality; but this, as I have explained, is only another form of violence, and so it must itself provoke more aggression. There is no way out for our sort of society, an unjust society must be violent. Any organization which denies the basic need for biological justice must become aggressive, even though it claims to be moral. This is true of most religions, which say that justice can only be obtained in another world, and not in this. It is also true of many movements for political reform.

Moralized aggression can, of course, be mixed with ordinary kindness and decency, so can the aggression of the social institutions it maintains. But aggression is so powerful (it was after all evolved to deal with desperate situations) that it decides the character of all people and institutions it infects. So through historical times our institutions have been aggressive, and because of this they make it even easier for aggressive people to get power and authority. That is why leaders – revolutionary as well as reactionary – so often behave worse than animals. I don't say this as invective – it is a sad, historical truth.

So human aggression has important features that make it more destructive than the aggression of other animals. It *is* animal aggression, but it has to be accommodated by our human minds, and presumably it appears to us as more alarming and frightening than it does to other animals. This is true of our subjective feelings of aggression as well as of the aggression we meet from outside. We have more complicated resources to deal with this increased vulnerability. When panic and fear become unbearable it is as if we lied and said they were not there, and out of this lie we build social morality. Children are especially vulnerable in this way, as I have said, but we are all exposed to the same pressures throughout our lives. As animals we react to threat in a natural, biological way; but we must also react in more complicated ways as human beings – mentally, emotionally and morally. It is because we cannot do this successfully that we no longer function as a species. Instead we have created all the things that threaten us: our military giantism, moral hysteria, industrial servitude, and all the ugly aggressiveness of a commercial culture.

Our situation has been made much worse, at least for the time being, by our technological success. The problem can now be described in this brief, schematic way.

We evolved in a biosphere but we live in what is more and more becoming a technosphere. We do not fit into it very well and so it activates our biological defences, one of which is aggression. Our environment is changing so rapidly that we cannot wait for biological solutions to evolve. So we should either change our technosphere or use technology to change human nature. But change in our society is really decided on urgent commercial imperatives, so nothing is done to solve our main problem. But a species living in an unfavourable environment dies out. For us the end will probably be quicker because the aggression we generate will be massively expressed through our technology.

This is very over-simplified and our fate is far from being so certain. But the combination of technology and socialized morality is very ugly, and it could lead to disaster. Alternatively, governments could begin to use technology to enforce socialized morality. That is by using drugs, selection, conditioning, genetics and so on, they could manufacture people who would fit into society. This would be just as disastrous. So if we do not want either of these things we must do something else. There are signs, in the search for counter-cultures and alternative politics, that we are beginning to do so.

What ought we to do? Live justly. But what is justice? Justice is allowing people to live in the way for which they evolved. Human beings have an emotional and physical need to do so, it is their biological expectation. They *can* only live in this way, or all the time struggle consciously or unconsciously to do so. That is the essential thing I want to say because it means that in fact our society and its morality, which deny this, and its technology which more and more prevents it, all the time whisper into people's ear 'You have no right to live'. That is what lies under the splendour of the modern world. Equality, freedom and fraternity must be reinterpreted in the light of this – otherwise real revolutionary change is impossible.

We can express this basic need in many ways: aesthetic, intellectual, the need to love, create, protect and enjoy. These are not higher things that can be added when more basic needs are met. *They* are basic. They must be the way in which we express all our existence, and if they do not control our daily life then we cannot function as human beings at all. They are not weakness, but they have nothing to do with the caricatures that pass for strength in our society – the hysterical old maids who become sergeant majors, the disguised peeping Toms who become moralists, the immature social misfits who become judges. Society pays lip service to these needs, but it has no real interest in them, and they are of course incompatible with the strident competitiveness of a commercial culture. So really we deny them. Like ghosts we teach a dead religion, build a few more prisons to worship Caesar in, and leave it at that. Blake said that when we try to become more than men we become less than beasts, and that is what we have done. Our human emotions and intellects are not things that stand apart from the long development of evolution; it is as animals we make our highest demands, and in responding to them as men we create our deepest human experience.

I have not answered many of the questions I have raised, but I have tried to explain things that often go unnoticed but which must be put right if anything is to work for us. They are difficult to put right because reforms easily become socially moralized. It is so easy to subordinate justice to power, but when this happens power takes on the dynamics and dialectics of aggression, and then nothing is really changed. Marx did not know about this problem and Lenin discovered it when it was too late.

There is no need for pessimism or resignation, and this play is certainly not either of these things. Lear is blind till they take his eyes away, and by then he has begun to see, to understand. (Blindness is a dramatic metaphor for insight, that is why Gloucester, Oedipus and Tiresias are blind.) Lear's new world is strange and so at first he can only grope painfully and awkwardly. Lear is old by then, but most of the play's audiences will be younger. It might seem to them that the truth is always ground for pessimism when it is discovered, but one soon comes to see it as an opportunity. Then you don't have to go on doing things that never work in the hope that they might one day – because now you know why they *can't*. Even bourgeois politics is more efficient than that.

Finally, I have not tried to say what the future should be like, because that is a mistake. If your plan of the future is too rigid you start to coerce people to fit into it. We do not need a plan of the future, we need a *method* of change.

I want to say something brief about the play. Lear did not have to destroy his daughters' innocence, he does so only because he doesn't understand his situation. When he does understand he leaves Thomas and Susan unharmed. But I think he had to destroy the innocent boy. Some things were lost to us long ago as a species, but we all seem to have to live through part of the act of losing them. We have to learn to do this without guilt or rancour or callousness – or socialized morality. So Lear's ghost isn't one of the angry ghosts from *Early Morning*, but something different.

Apart from the ten or so main characters of the play there are about seventy other speaking parts. In a sense these are one role showing the character of a society.

Act One shows a world dominated by myth. Act Two shows the clash between myth and reality, between superstitious men and the autonomous world. Act Three shows a resolution of this, in the world we prove real by dying in it.

Lear lived about the year 3100. He was king for 60 years. He built Leicester and was buried under the River Soar. His father was killed while trying to fly over London. His youngest daughter killed herself when she fell from power.

(HOLINSHED and GEOFFREY OF MONMOUTH)

LEAR *was presented by the English Stage Company at the Royal Court Theatre on September 29th 1971 with the following cast:*

FOREMAN	Geoffrey Hinsliff
1ST WORKMAN	Matthew Guinness
2ND WORKMAN	Struan Rodger
3RD WORKMAN	Ron Pember
SOLDIER	Bob Hoskins
LEAR	Harry Andrews
BODICE	Carmel McSharry
FONTANELLE	Rosemary McHale
WARRINGTON	Anthony Douse
OLD COUNCILLOR	George Howe
ENGINEER	Gareth Hunt
FIRING SQUAD OFFICER	William Hoyland
BISHOP	Gareth Hunt
DUKE OF NORTH	Eric Allen
DUKE OF CORNWALL	Alec Heggie
SOLDIER A	Bob Hoskins
THE GRAVEDIGGER'S BOY	Mark McManus
THE GRAVEDIGGER'S BOY'S WIFE	Celestine Randall
CARPENTER	Oliver Cotton
SERGEANT	Bob Hoskins
SOLDIER D *at the Gravedigger's Boy's House*	Ray Barron
SOLDIER E *at the Gravedigger's Boy's House*	Geoffrey Hinsliff
SOLDIER F *at the Gravedigger's Boy's House*	Antony Milner
JUDGE	William Hoyland
USHER	Gareth Hunt
OLD SAILOR	Matthew Guinness

BEN, *a Prison Orderly*	Derek Carpenter
SOLDIER H *Guard in the Prison*	Geoffrey Hinsliff
SOLDIER I *Guard in the Prison*	Richard Howard
SOLDIER G *Guard in the Prison*	Bob Hoskins
OLD PRISON ORDERLY	Anthony Douse
WOUNDED REBEL SOLDIER	Matthew Guinness
BODICE'S AIDE (Major Pellet)	Struan Rodger
SOLDIER J *Convoy Escort*	Bob Hoskins
SOLDIER K *Convoy Escort*	Geoffrey Hinsliff
SOLDIER L *Convoy Escort*	Richard Howard
PRISONER 1	Struan Rodger
PRISONER 2	Ron Pember
PRISONER 3	Derek Carpenter
PRISONER 4, *later Prison Doctor*	William Hoyland
PRISON COMMANDANT	Gareth Hunt
SOLDIER M *Prison Guard*	Ray Barron
SOLDIER N *Prison Guard*	Matthew Guinness
SOLDIER O *Prison Guard*	Eric Allen
FARMER	Geoffrey Hinsliff
FARMER'S WIFE	Marjorie Yates
FARMER'S SON	Antony Milner
THOMAS	Alec Heggie
JOHN	Richard Howard
SUSAN	Diana Quick
SMALL MAN	Ron Pember
OFFICER	Gareth Hunt
A BOY	Ray Barron

OTHER SOLDIERS, WORKERS, STRANGERS, COURT OFFICIALS, GUARDS: Geoffrey Hinsliff, Matthew Guinness, Antony Milner, Ray Barron, Ron Pember, Eric Allen, Anthony Douse, Bob Hoskins, Richard Howard, Gareth Hunt, Derek Carpenter, Marjorie Yates, Struan Rodger.

Directed by William Gaskill   Costumes designed by Deirdre Clancy
Sets designed by John Napier   Lighting by Andy Phillips

Act One

SCENE ONE

Near the wall.
A stack of building materials – shovels, picks, posts and a tarpaulin.
Silence. Then (offstage) a sudden indistinct shout, a crash, shouts. A
FOREMAN *and* TWO WORKERS *carry on a* DEAD WORKER *and*
put him down. They are followed by a SOLDIER.

FIRST WORKER. Get some water! He needs water.

FOREMAN. He's dead.

SOLDIER. Move 'im then!

FOREMAN. Get his legs.

SOLDIER (*to* FOREMAN). Can yer see 'em? Look an' see! They're
comin' up the ditch on the other side.

> FOREMAN *goes upstage to look off.* THIRD *and* FOURTH
> WORKERS *come on.*

THIRD WORKER (*coming on*). I shouted to him to run.

FOREMAN (*coming downstage*). Go back, go back! Work!

> FOURTH WORKER *goes off again.*

THIRD WORKER. You heard me shout!

FIRST WORKER. He says he's dead.

FOREMAN. Work!

SOLDIER (*to* FIRST WORKER). You! – make yerself responsible
for 'andin' in 'is pick t' stores. (*Suddenly he sees something off
stage and runs down to the others.*) Cover 'im! Quick!

FOREMAN (*points to tarpaulin*). Take that!

> *They cover the body with the tarpaulin.* LEAR, LORD
> WARRINGTON, *an* OLD COUNCILLOR, *an* OFFICER, *an*
> ENGINEER *and* LEAR'S DAUGHTERS – BODICE *and*

FONTANELLE – *come on. The* SOLDIER, FOREMAN *and*
WORKERS *stand stiffly.* WARRINGTON *signs to them and they*
work by the tarpaulin.

BODICE (*to* FONTANELLE). We needn't go on. We can see the
end.

ENGINEER. The chalk ends here. We'll move faster now.

COUNCILLOR (*looking at his map*). Isn't it a swamp on this map?

FONTANELLE (*to* BODICE). My feet are wet.

LEAR (*points to tarpaulin*). What's that?

ENGINEER. Materials for the –

WARRINGTON (*to* FOREMAN). Who is it?

FOREMAN. Workman.

WARRINGTON. What?

FOREMAN. Accident, sir.

LEAR. Who left that wood in the mud?

ENGINEER. That's just delivered. We're moving that to –

LEAR. It's been rotting there for weeks. (*To* WARRINGTON.)
They'll never finish! Get more men on it. The officers must
make the men work!

BODICE (*shakes* ENGINEER'*s hand*). Our visit has been so enjoyable
and informative.

FONTANELLE. Such an interesting day.

WARRINGTON. We can't take more men. The countryside would
be left derelict and there'd be starvation in the towns.

LEAR. Show me this body.

WARRINGTON *and the* SOLDIER *lift the tarpaulin.*

Blow on the head.

FOREMAN. Axe.

LEAR. What?

FOREMAN. An axe, sir. Fell on him.

LEAR. It's a flogging crime to delay work. (*To* WARRINGTON.)
You must deal with this fever. They treat their men like cattle.
When they finish work they must be kept in dry huts. All these
huts are wet. You waste men.

COUNCILLOR (*making a note*). I'll appoint a hut inspector.

LEAR. They dug the wall up again last night.

OFFICER. Local farmers. We can't catch them, they scuttle back home so fast.

LEAR. Use spring traps. (*To* FOREMAN.) Who dropped the axe?

WARRINGTON (*to* FOREMAN). Be quick!

FOREMAN *and* SOLDIER *push* THIRD WORKER *forward*.

LEAR. Court martial him. Fetch a firing squad. A drumhead trial for sabotage.

Quiet murmur of surprise. The OFFICER *goes to fetch the* FIRING SQUAD.

FONTANELLE. My feet are wet.

BODICE. She'll catch cold, father.

LEAR. Who was a witness?

WARRINGTON (*points to* FOREMAN). You!

FOREMAN. He dropped a pickaxe on his head. I've had my eye on him, sir. Always idle and –

LEAR (*to* THIRD WORKER). Prisoner of war?

FOREMAN. No. One of our men. A farmer.

LEAR. I understand! He has a grudge. I took him off his land.

The FIRING SQUAD *is marched in by the* OFFICER.

OFFICER. Squad as a squad – halt!

LEAR. I shall give evidence. He killed a workman on the wall. That alone makes him a traitor. But there's something else suspicious about him. Did you dig up the wall last night?

BODICE (*sighing*). It can easily be checked if he missed their roll calls.

LEAR. I started this wall when I was young. I stopped my enemies in the field, but there were always more of them. How could we ever be free? So I built this wall to keep our enemies out. My people will live behind this wall when I'm dead. You may be governed by fools but you'll always live in peace. My wall will make you free. That's why the enemies on our borders – the Duke of Cornwall and the Duke of North – try to stop us building it. I won't ask him which he works for – they're both hand in glove. Have him shot.

THIRD WORKER. Sir.

FONTANELLE (*aside to* BODICE). Thank God we've thought of ourselves.

OFFICER. Squad as a squad to firing positions – move!

LEAR (*indicating the* FIRING SQUAD). They must work on the wall, they're slow enough. (*Turns to* WARRINGTON.) See this is done. I'm going down to the swamp.

BODICE. Father, if you kill this man it will be an injustice.

LEAR. My dear, you want to help me, but you must let me deal with the things I understand. Listen and learn.

BODICE. What is there to learn? It's silly to make so much out of nothing. There was an accident. That's all.

LEAR (*half aside to her*). Of course there was an accident. But the work's slow. I must do something to make the officers move. That's what I came for, otherwise my visit's wasted. And there *are* saboteurs and there *is* something suspicious about this man –

BODICE. But think of the people! They already say you act like a schoolboy or an old spinster –

LEAR. Why are they waiting? It's cruel to make him wait.

OFFICER ⎱   Sir – you're –
WARRINGTON ⎰   Move, sir.

> LEAR *moves out of the* FIRING SQUAD'*s way.*

BODICE (*loudly*). Listen to me. All of you notice I disassociate myself from this act.

LEAR. Be quiet, Bodice. You mustn't talk like that in front of me.

FONTANELLE. And I agree with what my sister says.

LEAR. O my poor children, you're too good for this world. (*To the others*.) You see how well they'll govern when I'm dead. Bodice, you're right to be kind and merciful, and when I'm dead you *can* be – because you will have my wall. You'll live inside a fortress. Only I'm not free to be kind or merciful. I must build the fortress.

BODICE. How petty it is to be obstinate over nothing.

LEAR. I have explained and now you must understand!

BODICE. It is small and petty to make –

LEAR. I have explained.

BODICE. Small and petty! All these things are in your head. The Duke of Cornwall is not a monster. The Duke of North has not sworn to destroy you. I have proof of what I say.

LEAR. They're my sworn enemies. I killed the fathers therefore the sons must hate me. And when I killed the fathers I stood on the field among our dead and swore to kill the sons! I'm too old now, they've fooled me. But they won't take my country and dig my bones up when I'm dead. Never.

FONTANELLE (*to* BODICE). This is the moment to tell him.

BODICE. I'm going to marry the Duke of North and my sister's going to marry the Duke of Cornwall.

FONTANELLE. He's good and reliable and honest, and I trust him as if we'd been brought up together.

BODICE. Good lord! – how can they be your friends if you treat them like enemies? That's why they threatened you: it was political necessity. Well, now that's all in the past! We've brought them into your family and you can pull this absurd wall down. There! (*Slight laugh.*) You don't have to make your people slaves to protect you from your sons-in-law.

LEAR. My sons-in-law?

FONTANELLE. Congratulate us, father, give us your blessing.

BODICE. I'm marrying North.

FONTANELLE. And I'm marrying Cornwall.

LEAR (*points to* THIRD WORKER). Tie him straight! He's falling!

BODICE. So now you don't have to shoot him. Our husbands could never allow you to, anyway.

FONTANELLE. I know you'll get on with my husband. He's very understanding, he knows how to deal with old people.

LEAR. Straighter!

BODICE. You'll soon learn to respect them like your sons.

LEAR. I have no sons! I have no daughters! (*Tries to be calmer.*) Tell me – (*Stops, bewildered.*) – you are marrying North and you are marrying –. No, no! They've deceived you. You haven't met them. When did you meet them? Behind my back?

FONTANELLE. We sent each other photographs and letters. I can tell a man from his expression.

LEAR. O now I understand! You haven't met them. You're like blind children. Can't you see they only want to get over the wall? They'll be like wolves in a fold.

BODICE. Wall, wall, wall! This wall must be pulled down!

FONTANELLE. Certainly. My husband insists on that as part of the marriage contract.

BODICE (*to* OFFICER). I order you not to shoot this man. Our husbands will shoot anyone who shoots him. They offer us peace, we can't shoot innocent men because we think they're their spies!

LEAR. Shoot him!

BODICE. No!

LEAR. This is not possible! I must be obeyed!

WARRINGTON. Sir, this is out of hand. Nothing's gained by being firm in little matters. Keep him under arrest. The Privy Council will meet. There are more important matters to discuss.

LEAR. My orders are not little matters! What duke are you marrying? Who have you sold me to?

BODICE. If the king will not act reasonably it's your legal duty to disobey him.

WARRINGTON. Ma'am, you make this worse. Let me –

LEAR (*takes pistol from the* OFFICER *and threatens the* FIRING SQUAD). Shoot him!

BODICE. There, it's happened. Well, the doctors warned us, of course. (*Loudly.*) My father isn't well. Warrington, take the king back to his camp.

FONTANELLE. He shouldn't have come out today. This mud's too much for him. My feet are wringing.

LEAR. My enemies will not destroy my work! I gave my life to
these people. I've seen armies on their hands and knees in
blood, insane women feeding dead children at their empty
breasts, dying men spitting blood at me with their last breath,
our brave young men in tears –. But I could bear all this! When
I'm dead my people will live in freedom and peace and remember my name, no – venerate it! . . . They are my sheep and if
one of them is lost I'd take fire to hell to bring him out. I loved
and cared for all my children, and now you've sold them to their
enemies! (*He shoots* THIRD WORKER, *and his body slumps for-
wards on the post in a low bow.*) There's no more time, it's too
late to learn anything.

BODICE. Yes, you'll ruin yourself. Our husbands can't let you
terrorize these people – they'll be *their* people soon. They must
protect them from your madness.

LEAR. Work! Get your men to work! Get them on the wall!

> WORKERS, SOLDIERS *and* FOREMAN *go out. They take the
> two bodies with them.*

I knew it would come to this! I knew you were malicious! I built
my wall against *you* as well as my other enemies! You talk of
marriage? You have murdered your family. There will be no
more children. Your husbands are impotent. That's not an
empty insult. You wrote? My spies know more than that! You
will get nothing from this crime. You have perverted lusts. They
won't be satisfied. It *is* perverted to want your pleasure where it
makes others suffer. I pity the men who share your beds. I've
watched you scheme and plan – they'll lie by you when you
dream! Where will your ambition end? You will throw old men
from their coffins, break children's legs, pull the hair from old
women's heads, make young men walk the streets in beggary
and cold while their wives grow empty and despair – I am
ashamed of my tears! You have done this to me. The people will
judge between you and me.

LEAR *goes out. The* ENGINEER *and the* OLD COUNCILLOR *follow him.*

WARRINGTON. I'm sorry, ma'am. If you'd spoken another time –
FONTANELLE. You should have taken him away when you were told –
BODICE. You were caught out. Well, learn your lesson. As it happens, no harm's done. Go and keep in with him. We'll let you know what must happen next.

> WARRINGTON *and the others go out.* BODICE *and* FONTANELLE *are left alone.*

We must go to our husbands tonight.
FONTANELLE. Happiness at last! I was always terrified of him.
BODICE. We must attack before the wall's finished. I'll talk to my husband and you talk to yours. The four of us will sit in the Council of War. We must help each other. Goodbye.
FONTANELLE. Goodbye.

> *The daughters go out.*

SCENE TWO

Parade ground.
A saluting stand. LEAR, OLD COUNCILLOR, WARRINGTON, BISHOP, MILITARY AIDES. *Marching, march music, and parade commands are heard during the scene.* LEAR *stands with both arms stretched out in a gesture of salute and blessing.*

LEAR. Greetings to the eighth regiment! (*Still saluting. To* WARRINGTON.) You will command my right flank and circle them on the right. Then I attack the centre. That's how I crushed the fathers. (*Still saluting.*) I salute my loyal comrades!
WARRINGTON. We could refuse this war. We're old, sir. We could retire and let these young men choose what to do with

their own lives. Ask your daughters to let you live quietly in the country.

LEAR (*still saluting*). How could I trust myself to them? My daughters are proclaimed outlaws, without rights of prisoners of war. They can be raped – or murdered. Why should they be held for trial? Their crimes aren't covered by my laws. Where does their vileness come from?

WARRINGTON. I've given you advice it was my duty to give. But I'm proud you've rejected it.

LEAR (*still saluting*). Greetings to my glorious ninth!

WARRINGTON. I have two letters from your daughters, sir. They both wrote in secret and told me not to let anyone know, especially each other.

LEAR. Give them to me.

WARRINGTON. No, sir. They ask me to betray you and then each other. They'll both make me head of the army and let me share their bed.

LEAR. They live in their own fantasies! They chose their husbands well, they should be married to my enemies! Have the ceremonies taken place? It doesn't matter. (*He takes the letters from* WARRINGTON. *He reads part of one.*) 'He is mad. If he won what security would you have?' (*He reads from the other.*) 'He would turn on you as he turned on us.' (*Salutes as before.*) Greetings to my friends the ninth! (*Still saluting.*) Warrington, if I'm killed or fall into their hands you must take my place and build the wall.

WARRINGTON. Sir. This fry won't take you. Your army is paraded!

BISHOP. Our prayers go with you into war, sir. God blesses the righteous. He has nothing to do with women who make war.

COUNCILLOR. I feel confidence in my bones. That's never failed me. If only I were a young man!

LEAR. The trumpet! I smell victory!

Cheers and trumpet. They go out.

SCENE THREE

Daughters' War Council.
Table, chairs, map. BODICE, FONTANELLE, NORTH, CORNWALL.
BODICE *knits.*

NORTH. We share the command between us.
CORNWALL. Yes.
NORTH. We must guess how Lear will attack.
BODICE (*knitting*). He'll send Warrington round the right and attack the centre himself.
CORNWALL. Are you sure, sister?
BODICE. He always has and he's set in his ways.

> CORNWALL, NORTH *and* BODICE *study the map.* BODICE *knits at the same time.*

FONTANELLE (*aside*). I'm bitterly disappointed in my husband. How dare he! A civil servant wrote his letters and an actor posed for his photographs. When he gets on top of me I'm so angry I have to count to ten. That's long enough. Then I wait till he's asleep and work myself off. I'm not making do with that for long. I've written to Warrington and told him to use all his men against Bodice and leave my army alone – that'll finish her – and then I paid a young, blond lieutenant on my husband's staff to shoot him while they're busy fighting. Then I'll marry Warrington and let him run the country for me.
NORTH (*studying the map*). They can't get round these mountains.
CORNWALL. No.
BODICE (*aside*). I'm not disappointed in my husband. I expected nothing. There is some satisfaction in listening to him squeak on top of me while he tries to get his little paddle in. I lie still and tell myself while he whines, you'll pay for this, my lad. He sees me smiling and contented and thinks it's his virility. Virility! It'd be easier to get blood out of a stone, and far more probable. I've bribed a major on his staff to shoot him in the

battle – they're all corrupt – and I've written to Warrington and told him to use all his force against hers. She'll be crushed and then I'll marry Warrington and run the country through him. So I shall have three countries: my father's, my husband's and my sister and brother-in-law's.

NORTH. Till tomorrow.

CORNWALL. Yes. (*Goes to* FONTANELLE.) Let's go to bed. I need your body before I risk death.

FONTANELLE. My darling. (*Aside.*) I'll get him drunk. He's such a frightened little boy, fighting terrifies him. He'll fidget and mawl all night. I'd rather mop up his vomit.

NORTH (*to* BODICE). Let me take you to bed, my dear. I must feel you on me when I go to the field.

BODICE. Yes, North. (*Aside.*) He must prove himself a man before he plays with his soldiers. He'll fuss and try all night, but he won't be able to raise his standard. I'll help him and make it worse. By the morning he won't know which side he's fighting on. And that'll make it easier for the major.

FONTANELLE. Sleep well.

BODICE. And you.

They all go out.

SCENE FOUR

Prison area.
THREE SOLDIERS (A, B *and* C) *upstage.*

SOLDIER A. 'Ow long they goin' a keep us 'ere? The war's over. They wan'a send us 'ome.

SOLDIER B. They'll think a some reason. (*Indicates offstage.*) Watered 'im yet?

SOLDIER A. No point.

BODICE, FONTANELLE *and an* OFFICER *hurry on downstage.*

BODICE. Is our father taken yet?

OFFICER. He got away.

FONTANELLE (*stamps her foot*). Damn! That's spoiled everything!

CORNWALL *comes on.*

(*Aside.*) My husband! Damn! Damn! Damn! Has the lieutenant dared to betray me?

CORNWALL (*kisses* FONTANELLE). A great victory! They fought like devils but we beat them!

BODICE (*aside*). If I hadn't told him father's plans he'd be lying dead under his army by now.

NORTH *comes in.*

(*Aside.*) Damn it! My husband!

NORTH (*kisses* BODICE). Your enemies are routed!

FONTANELLE (*to* CORNWALL. *Prying*). What are our losses? Are your staff all safe?

NORTH. I lost one major. He was talking to one of Cornwall's lieutenants before the fighting –

CORNWALL. A young blond man called Crag.

FONTANELLE. Yes, I knew him.

CORNWALL. – the first shell fell between them and blew their heads off.

BODICE (*aside*). One can't allow for everything.

NORTH. Warrington's in the cage.

BODICE (*aside*). Now I must be careful. He didn't attack my sister's men, so I couldn't risk him talking about my letter. I had his tongue cut out.

CORNWALL. Let's go and see what he has to say for himself.

FONTANELLE. Wait . . . (NORTH *and* CORNWALL *stop.*) He was shouting insults about you and I didn't want our troops to be upset. So I let them cut his tongue out. I thought that was best.

CORNWALL. O, my men would have laughed at him.

BODICE (*aside*). I see my sister thinks like me, I must never trust her.

NORTH. It doesn't matter, he's going to be killed anyway.

BODICE. I'll see to that for you. Go and thank our armies. (*Aside.*) He could still make signs. It's better if he dies in silence.

NORTH. Yes, Cornwall, let's go together.

CORNWALL *and* NORTH *go out with the* OFFICER.

BODICE. I'm glad they've gone. Men are squeamish after a war. (*To* SOLDIER A.) Private, you look strong and capable, would you like to go up in the world?

SOLDIER A. Yessam.

FONTANELLE. Good teeth, too.

BODICE. Get rid of them.

SOLDIER A *flicks his head and* SOLDIERS B *and* C *go out.*

Fetch him out.

SOLDIER A *fetches* WARRINGTON *on stage. He is dishevelled, dirty and bound.*

SOLDIER A. Yer wan' 'im done in in a fancy way? Thass sometimes arst for. I once 'ad t' cut a throat for some ladies t' see once.

FONTANELLE. It's difficult to choose.

BODICE (*sits on her riding stick and takes out her knitting*). Let him choose. (*Knits.*)

SOLDIER A. I once give a 'and t' flay a man. I couldn't manage that on me own. Yer need two at least for that. Shall I beat 'im up?

FONTANELLE. You're all talk! Wind and piss!

SOLDIER A. Juss for a start. Don't get me wrong, thass juss for a start. Get it goin' and see 'ow it goes from there.

FONTANELLE. But I want something –

BODICE (*knitting*). O shut up and let him get on with it. (*Nods at* SOLDIER A *to go on.*)

SOLDIER A. Thankyermum. Right, less see 'ow long it takes t' turn yer inside out.

FONTANELLE. Literally?

SOLDIER A (*hits* WARRINGTON). O, 'e wants it the 'ard way.
(*Hits him.*) Look at 'im puttin' on the officer class! (*Hits him.*)
Don't pull yer pips on me, laddie.

FONTANELLE. Use the boot! (SOLDIER A *kicks him.*) Jump on
him! (*She pushes* SOLDIER A.) Jump on his head!

SOLDIER A. Lay off, lady, lay off! 'Oo's killin' 'im, me or you?

BODICE (*knits*). One plain, two pearl, one plain.

FONTANELLE. Throw him up and drop him. I want to hear him
drop.

SOLDIER A. Thass a bit 'eavy, yer need proper gear t' drop 'em –

FONTANELLE. Do something! Don't let him get away with it. O
Christ, why did I cut his tongue out? I want to hear him
scream!

SOLDIER A (*jerks* WARRINGTON'*s head up*). Look at 'is eyes, Miss.
Thass boney-fidey sufferin'.

FONTANELLE. O yes, tears and blood. I wish my father was
here. I wish he could see him. Look at his hands! Look at
them going! What's he praying or clutching? Smash his
hands!

> SOLDIER A *and* FONTANELLE *jump on* WARRINGTON'*s
> hands.*

Kill his hands! Kill his feet! Jump on it – all of it! He can't hit
us now. Look at his hands like boiling crabs! Kill it! Kill all of
it! Kill him inside! Make him dead! Father! Father! I want to
sit on his lungs!

BODICE (*knits*). Plain, pearl, plain. She was just the same at
school.

FONTANELLE. I've always wanted to sit on a man's lungs. Let me.
Give me his lungs.

BODICE (*to* SOLDIER A). Down on your knees.

SOLDIER A. Me?

BODICE. Down! (SOLDIER A *kneels.*) Beg for his life.

SOLDIER A (*confused*). 'Is? (*Aside.*) What a pair! – O spare 'im,
mum.

BODICE (*knits*). No.

SOLDIER A. If yer could see yer way to. 'E's a poor ol' gent, lonely ol' bugger.

BODICE. It can't be pearl? I think there's an error in this pattern book.

FONTANELLE. O let me sit on his lungs. Get them out for me.

BODICE. I shall refuse his pardon. That always gives me my deepest satisfaction. Hold him up.

SOLDIER A *sits* WARRINGTON *upright*.

FONTANELLE. Look at his mouth! He wants to say something. I'd die to listen. O why did I cut his tongue out?

SOLDIER A. 'E's wonderin' what comes next. Yer can tell from 'is eyes.

BODICE (*pulls the needles from her knitting and hands the knitting to* FONTANELLE). Hold that and be careful.

SOLDIER A. Look at 'is eyes!

BODICE. It's my duty to inform you –

SOLDIER A. Keep still! Keep yer eyes on madam when she talks t'yer.

BODICE. – that your pardon has been refused. He can't talk or write, but he's cunning – he'll find some way of telling his lies. We must shut him up inside himself. (*She pokes the needles into* WARRINGTON'*s ears*.) I'll just jog these in and out a little. Doodee, doodee, doodee, doo.

FONTANELLE. He can see my face but he can't hear me laugh!

BODICE. Fancy! Like staring into a silent storm.

FONTANELLE. And now his eyes.

BODICE. No . . . I think not. (*To* SOLDIER A.) Take him out in a truck and let him loose. Let people know what happens when you try to help my father. (*To* FONTANELLE.) Let me sit on his lungs! You old vulture! Go and flap round the battlefield.

FONTANELLE. Don't make fun of me. You're so stupid. You don't understand anything.

BODICE. I don't think I'd like to understand you. (*Takes her*

knitting from FONTANELLE.) You've let my knitting run!
(*Starts to go.*) Come on, we've won the war but we can't dilly-
dally, there's still part of the day left. I must see what my
husband's up to.

> BODICE *and* FONTANELLE *go out.* SOLDIER A *starts to take*
> WARRINGTON *out.*

SOLDIER A. It's all over. Walking offal! Don't blame me, I've got
a job t' do. If we was fightin' again t'morra I could end up
envyin' you anytime. Come on then, less 'ave yer. Yer'll live if
yer want to.

> *They go out.*

SCENE FIVE

Woods.
*A large empty plate and jug on the bare stage. Further down, a piece
of bread.* LEAR *and the* OLD COUNCILLOR *come in. They are
ragged, tired, dirty and frightened.*

COUNCILLOR. I've studied people, sir. Your daughters aren't
bad. Put yourself in their hands. They'll respond to your trust.
LEAR. Never. (*Stops.*) A jug and a plate. Empty!
COUNCILLOR. At least there are people about! I thought this was
the end of the world. Wait here, sir, and I'll look.
LEAR. No, don't leave me!
COUNCILLOR. There might be a village and I can get some food.
I'll be careful, sir. Sit down and rest.

> OLD COUNCILLOR *goes out.* LEAR *finds the bread on the
> ground.*

LEAR. Bread! Someone was eating this and they dropped it and
ran away. (*He eats it.*) That's all there is.

> LEAR *sits down. He is very tired.* WARRINGTON *comes on
> upstage. He is crippled and his face looks as if it's covered with*

bad plastic surgery. He carries a knife awkwardly. He's already seen LEAR *and comes on creeping towards him from behind.*

My daughters have taken the bread from my stomach. They grind it with my tears and the cries of famished children – and eat. The night is a black cloth on their table and the stars are crumbs, and I am a famished dog that sits on the earth and howls. I open my mouth and they place an old coin on my tongue. They lock the door of my coffin and tell me to die. My blood seeps out and they write in it with a finger. I'm old and too weak to climb out of this grave again.

WARRINGTON *sees someone coming and goes out.*

(*Looking off.*) Is this one of my daughters' men?

The GRAVEDIGGER'S BOY *comes on. He carries bread and water.*

No, there's no blood on him. – Who are you?
BOY. I live near here.
LEAR. Is that bread?
BOY. Yes.
LEAR. Is it poisoned?
BOY. No.
LEAR. Then my daughters didn't send him. They'd never miss a chance to poison good bread. Who's it for?
BOY. There's a man who roams round here. He's wild. They say he was wounded in the war.
LEAR. I'm hungry. I know you have no pity to sell, there's always a shortage of that in wartime, but you could sell me some bread. I can pay. (*Looks round.*) My friend keeps my money.
BOY. Take it. It's not much. (LEAR *eats.*) Have you come far?
LEAR. No.
BOY. Where are you going?
LEAR. I shan't know till I get there.
BOY. Was that your friend with the stick? He's left you, he wanted a horse to take him to town.

LEAR. The traitor! Give him a bad horse and let him break his neck!

BOY. I can't leave you out here on your own. I think you'd better come to my place for the night. Then you can think what to do.

LEAR. Your place? Have you any daughters?

BOY. No.

LEAR. Then I'll come. No daughters! Where he lives the rain can't be wet or the wind cold, and the holes cry out when you're going to tread in them.

The BOY *leads* LEAR *out.*

SCENE SIX

The GRAVEDIGGER'S BOY's *house.*
Wooden house upstage. A few steps to the front door. A well. A bench with bedding on it.
LEAR *and the* BOY *are sitting on the ground.*

BOY. My father was the village gravedigger. I liked to help him when I was a boy, and he taught me the work. He didn't want to be buried in a graveyard – you wouldn't want to be buried where you work.

The BOY'S WIFE *comes from the house with three bowls of soup. She gives the bowls out and sits by the* BOY. *The three eat.*

So when he died I found this place and started to dig his grave. And when I got down I struck a well. I thought, there's water here and some land, why do I want to dig graves all my life? So I live here and built this farm. (*Nods at bowl.*) It's good.

LEAR (*eating. To himself. The* BOY'S WIFE *stares at him*). The mouse comes out of his hole and stares. The giant wants to eat the dragon, but the dragon has grabbed the carving knife.

BOY. My wife keeps pigs. I've got two fields and I catch things. No one minds out here. Any more?

LEAR *shakes his head. The* WIFE *takes the bowls inside.*

Now the nights are hot we've started to sleep outside. You can sleep inside if you like.

LEAR. I can't sleep on my own since I lost my army.

BOY. Then sleep out here. (*Indicates well.*) The well went dry in the summer. I had to dig down again. But it's all right now, I'm down to the spring.

LEAR (*to himself*). My daughters turned a dog out of its kennel because it got fond of its sack.

BOY. The pigs don't cost anything, I let them grub round all day and lock them up at night. They fatten themselves and I just have to slaughter them. Would you like a walk? I'll show you where we keep them. And then we must get to bed. I'm up early in the mornings. (*They stand. He calls into the house.*) Won't be long. Can you fetch the spare blanket? (*To* LEAR.) Take my arm.

LEAR. No. I once knew a man who was drowned on a bridge in a flood.

LEAR *and the* BOY *go out. After a moment* WARRINGTON *comes on, still holding the knife. He has been watching* LEAR *and he now stares after him. He sees a movement through the doorway and hides. The* WIFE *comes out of the house with a blanket. She cries quietly, persistently and evenly, as if out of habit. She sees* WARRINGTON.

WIFE. Go away! (*She throws the blanket at him.*) Beggars, scroungers, filthy old men!

She looks round for something to throw. She runs into the house, crying loudly. WARRINGTON *looks round in terror. He hides down the well. The* WIFE *comes out of the house with a soup bowl ready to throw. She can't see* WARRINGTON. *She sits down and cries loudly and bitterly.*
The BOY *runs in.*

BOY. What is it? Are you all right?

WIFE (*crying*). Your wild man was here!

BOY. What did he do? Are you all right?

    LEAR *walks in*.

LEAR. There's no one here.

WIFE (*crying*). Of course not! He ran away.

BOY. Don't cry.

WIFE (*crying*). I'm trying to stop.

BOY. He only wanted his food. I'll go up and feed him in the
morning. Look, come and lie down. You're shivering. (*He
spreads the blanket and pillow for her*.) Let me cover you up.

    She lies down. She cries more quietly.

That's better. (*To* LEAR.) It's because she's carrying.

LEAR. Poor woman.

BOY (*taking* LEAR *to the other side of the stage*). We'd all better
go to sleep, we don't want to disturb her. You can sleep here.
(*He spreads a blanket and pillow*.) You'll be fine here. Good
night.

    BOY *goes back to his* WIFE *and lies beside her*. LEAR *sits on his
blanket*.

LEAR (*to himself*). It is night. My daughters empty their prisons
and feed the men to the dead in their graveyards. The wolf
crawls away in terror and hides with the rats. Hup, prince! Hup
rebel! Do tricks for human flesh! When the dead have eaten
they go home to their pits and sleep. (*He lies down in an awkward
pose and sleeps*.)

WIFE (*crying*). Hold me. Stop me crying.

BOY (*holding her*). You must take things easy now. You work too
hard.

WIFE. Don't say that! It's not true!

BOY. All right, I won't.

WIFE. But you don't believe me.

BOY. Yes I do.

WIFE. You don't. I can see you don't. Why can't I make you happy?

BOY. I am happy.

WIFE. You're not. I know you're not. You make me happy – my father said I'd be unhappy here, but I'm not, you've made me so happy – why can't I make you happy? Look at the way you brought that man here! The first one you find! Why? I'm so afraid something will happen.

BOY. Does he matter to you?

WIFE. Of course he matters! And he's a tramp!

BOY. I'll make him wash.

WIFE. You see! You don't understand! Who is he?

BOY. I don't know. He told me he was an officer, but that's not true. Who'd take their orders from him!

WIFE. And he talks to himself. I'm afraid of him.

BOY. That's only a habit. He's lonely. You'll be all right, I thought you'd like someone to help you. He can look after the pigs.

WIFE. I knew it! You're going to ask him to stay!

BOY. What else can I do? He can't look after himself. He's a poor old man – how can I throw him out? Who'd look after him then? I won't do it!

WIFE. O you're a fool! Can anyone come who likes? Don't you have any sense of responsibility?

BOY. Responsibility!

LEAR. . . . When he saluted I saw blood on his hand . . .

WIFE. Listen!

LEAR. . . . I slept in the morning because all the birds were dead . . .

WIFE. . . . He's stopped.

BOY. O go to sleep. Please. For the child's sake.

Silence. They all sleep. WARRINGTON *comes out of the well. He still carries the knife. He goes to the* BOY *and his* WIFE *and peers down to see who they are. He crosses to* LEAR *and stops.*

Peers. Throws himself on LEAR, *roars, and hits him with the knife.* LEAR *jumps up.*

LEAR (*still dreaming*). My daughters – help me! There! Guards! (*Grabs* WARRINGTON *and stares at his face.*) What's this? . . . No! No!

The BOY *runs to* LEAR *and* WARRINGTON *runs out.*

A ghost!
BOY. He's gone! He ran!
LEAR. A ghost!
WIFE. It's the wild man! I saw him!
BOY. A light! (*The* WIFE *runs into the house.*) He's bleeding! Water! Cloth! (*To* LEAR.) Your arm! It's cut.
LEAR. He's dead! I saw his face! It was like a stone! I shall die!

The WIFE *comes out with a light.*

BOY. Water –
WIFE. Bring him inside! It's not safe out here!
BOY (*helping* LEAR *into the house*). Yes. Fetch the blanket. Quick. He's bleeding.
LEAR. I'll die! I've seen a ghost. I'm going to die. That's why he came back. I'll die.
BOY. The steps.

> BOY *takes* LEAR *into the house. His* WIFE *picks up the blankets and follows them in.*

SCENE SEVEN

Same.
The next afternoon. There is no one there. The BOY *comes in. Takes off his hat and hangs it up on the side of the house. His* WIFE *comes in from the opposite side. She carries a pig pole and an empty swill bucket.*

WIFE. Is he still asleep?

BOY. I don't know. I just got back.

WIFE. You haven't asked him about last night.

BOY. Not yet. (*He kisses her.*) You're better.

WIFE. Yes. (*She takes the pole and bucket to the side of the house.*) The well's dirty, I saw it this morning when I did the washing.

BOY. O lord! I'll go down later on.

> The CARPENTER *comes in. He is tall and dark and carries a wooden box.*

Hello.

CARPENTER. Hello.

BOY. How are you!

CARPENTER. Fine. A bit busy.

BOY (*points to box*). What is it?

CARPENTER. Something I made.

BOY. It's early, but I'll go and shut the pigs up.

> The BOY *goes out.*

WIFE. What is it?

CARPENTER. A cradle. (*He gives it to her.*)

WIFE. O.

CARPENTER. He doesn't mind.

WIFE. It's beautiful.

> The CARPENTER *sits and looks at her. Slight pause.*

He's got someone staying here. An old man. You haven't seen him in the village?

CARPENTER. No. Who is he? I'll try and find out.

WIFE. He just brought him here to look after the pigs. Why? It's so silly, so silly . . .

CARPENTER (*after another slight pause*). Any jobs I can do?

WIFE. The door wants mending, but he'll do that.

CARPENTER. No, I left my tools in the cart down on the road. I'll fix it.

BOY (*off*). I-yoo! I-yoo! I-yoo! (*Two or three pigs squeal.*)

    LEAR *comes out of the house.*

LEAR (*puzzled*). I've slept all day. It's evening. (*Sees* CARPENTER.) Who's that?

WIFE. A man from the village.

LEAR. O. (*He sits on the cradle.*)

CARPENTER. ⎱ Not on that!
WIFE.   ⎰ You'll break it!

LEAR (*stands*). Where's your husband?

WIFE. He'll be here. I suppose you'll go away now after last night.

LEAR (*confused*). I don't know. I dreamed –

    The BOY *comes in.*

BOY. How are you? I thought I heard you up. Let me see your arm.

WIFE. John brought this.

BOY (*looks at the cradle*). O that's very clever. For the child. Thanks. (*The* CARPENTER *stands.*) You needn't go.

CARPENTER. Your wife wants me to fix her door.

    The CARPENTER *goes out. The* BOY *looks at* LEAR'S *cut.*

WIFE (*picking up the cradle*). It's not deep.

BOY. It needs washing.

    The WIFE *goes into the house with the cradle.*

LEAR. Who is he?

BOY. Village carpenter. He makes coffins and cradles and mends chairs, anything. He's very good. Don't worry about him, he's always hanging round. He's in love with my wife.

LEAR. Last night I saw a ghost.

BOY (*amused*). My father said there aren't any, and he should know. It was this wild man.

LEAR. I see, I see . . . then it was all in my dream. (*Slight pause.*) I should have spent my life here.

BOY (*looking at the cut*). I'm sorry about this.

LEAR (*still confused and puzzled*). I've been cut before. It's almost gone. I was worse when I came here. You've looked after me well. I slept like a child in this silence all day. It's so long since I slept like that, I'd forgotten ... And now I shall get well again. It's so simple and easy here. (*Becoming angry.*) But where shall I go now, how can I live, what will become of me?

BOY. Stay here. You can look after my pigs. I can't pay you but you can eat and sleep with us.

LEAR. No. I'd get you into trouble. No, no. I must go away.

BOY. Listen, how many men were you in charge of?

LEAR. A few.

BOY. Well they won't come all this way for one old man who was in charge of a few other men. So stay.

LEAR. I could have a new life here. I could forget all the things that frighten me – the years I've wasted, my enemies, my anger, my mistakes. I've been too trusting, too lenient! I'm tormented by regrets – I must forget it all, throw it away! Yes! – let me live here and work for you.

BOY. Good. You'll be a real help to me when you've settled in. I'll be able to clear some more fields. You needn't worry about the soldiers. They're too busy looking for the king to worry about you. Did you know they're pulling his wall down?

LEAR. The wall?

BOY. Up and down, up and down. The king was mad. He took all the men from this village. But I hid. They'd worked with their hands all their lives but when they started on the wall their hands bled for a week.

LEAR. No.

BOY. You died of work or they shot you for not working. There was a disease –

LEAR. They tried to stop that.

BOY. – 'Wall death'. Their feet used to swell with the mud. The stink of it even when you were asleep! Living in a grave! He should come here – I'd go back to my old job and dig a grave for him! We used to dig his wall up at nights, when they were working near here. (*Sighs.*) Let's talk about something else. (LEAR *stops listening to him.*) My wife will be all right. She'll be a bit cold at first, but she'll soon be glad to have you helping us . . . We're supposed to be a bad match. I know her father didn't want us to marry. He's never come to see us. I asked him. I don't like that, it makes you feel bad. He's a priest, he taught her everything. She's very clever, but she can't understand how I live. I've got my house, my farm, my wife – and every night I tell her I love her. How could I be unhappy? She's afraid it will change, she'd like to put a fence round us and shut everyone else out.

His WIFE *comes out of the house with a long rope. She fixes it across the back of the stage as a long clothes line. Short silence.*

LEAR. I remember some of my dream. There was a king and he had a fountain in his garden. It was as big as the sea. One night the fountain howled and in the morning the king went to look at it. It was red. The servants emptied it and under the sea they found a desert. The king looked in the sand and there was a helmet and sword.

The WIFE *goes into the house.*

So the king –
BOY. I know that. A clown told it to us at the fair.

LEAR *stares at him. The* WIFE *comes out of the house with a basket of washing.*

WIFE. I want some more water but it's dirty.
BOY (*stands*). I'll go down.

The WIFE *takes some pegs from the wall and starts to peg out a line of white sheets. The* BOY *climbs into the well and goes out of sight.*

LEAR (*to* WIFE). I'll do that. You mustn't work too hard.

She doesn't answer, but LEAR *helps her. They hang the sheets so that the bottoms just clear the ground.*

WIFE (*pegging*). Who is the wild man? You recognized him last night.

LEAR (*holding up a sheet*). No. I was dreaming.

WIFE (*taking the sheet*). When are you going?

LEAR (*picking up pegs*). Your husband's asked me to work for him.

WIFE (*pegging*). You're not stopping here. I won't have you.

LEAR (*handing her pegs*). He needs me. He said so.

WIFE (*taking the pegs*). I'm not having any dirty old tramps about. I'm carrying. I mustn't let myself get upset.

LEAR (*adjusting a sheet. Becoming angry*). You don't hang them straight.

WIFE (*pegging*). I could easily make him send you away.

LEAR. Straight.

WIFE (*pegging*). I don't want to have to do that. I'm not arguing and shouting any more, it upsets him too much. Please go – and don't tell him I made you.

LEAR (*holding up a sheet*). Where can I go?

WIFE (*taking the sheet*). Anywhere. You're free. You've got the whole world.

LEAR. He asked me to stay! No, I won't go! (*He crosses to the well.*) He said I could stay. He won't break his word. I'm too old to look after myself. I can't live in ditches and barns and beg for scraps and hire myself to peasants! No, I won't be at everyone's call! My daughters sent you! *You* go! It's you who're destroying this place! We must get rid of you! – (*He stops short and stares at the bucket.*)

WIFE. What is it?

LEAR. Blood.

WIFE. What?

LEAR. Blood. That's blood in the water. I've seen it before. (*Calls down the well.*) What are you doing? Where are you?

BOY (*off*). What?

WIFE. That's where he was hiding! (*Calls down well*.) He hid down there last night – (*To* LEAR.) – and then he came up and tried to kill you and ran away!

LEAR (*afraid*). No. There's too much blood . . . He came back and he's down there now . . .

    Silence. A SERGEANT *and* THREE SOLDIERS (D, E *and* F) *come on. They all carry rifles.*

SOLDIER D. Don't run. I don't like breakin' women's legs.

SERGEANT. Turn it over inside.

    SOLDIERS D *and* E *go into the house.*

'Oo else yer got knockin' around?

LEAR. No one. You want me. We can go now.

    He starts to go. SOLDIER F *stops him.*

No, no! We must go.

SOLDIER F. 'Oo else? Shouldn't lie your age, time yer knowd better.

SERGEANT. Come on, darlin', yer must a 'ad some one t' put yer in that class.

SOLDIER F. Couldn't a bin 'im.

    SOLDIER D *comes out of the house.*

SOLDIER D. 'E'd 'ave t' use a carrot.

SOLDIER F. 'E would, the dirty ol' toe rag.

WIFE. Go away –

SOLDIER D (*to* SERGEANT). Empty.

WIFE. – he's gone.

SERGEANT. 'Oo'd leave a nice little lay like you?

    SOLDIER E *comes from behind the house.*

SOLDIER E. Pigs out the back.

LEAR. I look after them!

SERGEANT. We know there's a young fella.

LEAR. There's no one else. Take me away.
BOY (*off*). He's here! I've got him!

The SOLDIERS *stare. They are puzzled.*

LEAR. We can go. The girl didn't know who I am. I'll report you
for –

SOLDIER F *puts his hand over* LEAR's *mouth. Silence.*

BOY (*off*). His neck's broken.

SOLDIER D *points to the well.*

SERGEANT (*threatens* LEAR *with his rifle*). Tell 'im somethin'.
LEAR (*speaking down the well*). Yes.
BOY (*off*). He's dead. I'll bring him up. Pull the rope.

The SERGEANT *pulls the rope. The* SOLDIERS *take the* WIFE
and hide behind the sheets with her.

(*Off. Nearer.*) Steady.

LEAR *goes upstage, sits on the steps or the bench and watches. The*
SERGEANT *goes behind the sheets. The* BOY *comes out of the well,*
carrying WARRINGTON. WARRINGTON *is dripping wet.*

He fell down. He must have died straight away. My God! –
he's breathing. There's bubbles on his mouth! Look! Help me!

He puts WARRINGTON *down. A pool forms round him. The*
BOY *looks at* LEAR. *Stops. Suddenly he panics and shouts.*

Cordelia!

The SERGEANT *and* SOLDIERS E *and* F *come from behind the*
sheets.

Cordelia!

SOLDIER E *shoots him. He staggers upstage towards the sheets.*
His head is down. He clutches a sheet and pulls it from the line.
CORDELIA *stands behind it. Her head is down and she covers*

her face with her hands. SOLDIER D *is preparing to rape her. The* BOY *turns slowly away and as he does so the sheet folds round him. For a second he stands in silence with the white sheet draped round him. Only his head is seen. It is pushed back in shock and his eyes and mouth are open. He stands rigid. Suddenly a huge red stain spreads on the sheet.*

SERGEANT. Kill the pigs.

> SOLDIER E *runs off.*

SOLDIER F (*peering down at* WARRINGTON). Chriss look at this!
SERGEANT (*to* SOLDIER D). Do that inside.
LEAR. She's pregnant.
SOLDIER D. It can play with the end.
SOLDIER F (*poking* WARRINGTON's *mouth with the end of his rifle*). Look at this blowin' bubbles!

> *Off, squealing starts as the pigs are slaughtered.* SOLDIER D *takes the* WIFE *into the house. The* BOY *suddenly drops dead.*

SERGEANT. Drop 'im down the 'ole.

> *The* SERGEANT *and* SOLDIER F *drop* WARRINGTON *down the well.*

SOLDIER F. 'Ere's another one.
SERGEANT. Up!

> *They drop the* BOY *down the well. He points to* LEAR.

An' run 'im down t' the truck.

> *The* SERGEANT *goes into the house.*

SOLDIER F. Some jammy bastards 'ave all the fun. I don't fancy old grandads.

> *Off, the pig squealing stops.*

LEAR (*stands*). O burn the house! You've murdered the husband, slaughtered the cattle, poisoned the well, raped the mother,

killed the child – you must burn the house! You're soldiers –
you must do your duty! My daughters expect it! O burn the
house! Burn the house! Burn the house!

SOLDIER F. Shut it an' move.

> SOLDIER F *takes* LEAR *outside.* SOLDIER E *comes on from
> behind the house.*

LEAR (*going*). O burn it down! Burn it!

> *There is blood on* SOLDIER E's *face, neck, hands, clothes and
> boots. In the house* CORDELIA *gives a high, short gasp.*

SOLDIER E (*muttering contentedly*). An' I'll 'ave 'er reekin' a pig
blood. Somethin' t' write 'ome t' tell mother.

> *The* CARPENTER *follows him on. He carries his tool pack. He
> takes a cold chisel from it.*

(*Sees* CARPENTER.) Yes? (*A fraction later he calls towards the
house.*) Sarge!

> *The* CARPENTER *kills him with a blow from the cold chisel.*

CARPENTER (*looks towards the house*). Are there more of you?

> *The* CARPENTER *picks up* SOLDIER D's *rifle and goes into the
> house. Slight pause. Three rifle shots from inside the house.
> Silence.*

Act Two

SCENE ONE

Courtroom.
NORTH *and* CORNWALL *enter and talk quietly together while the court assembles. There is a* JUDGE, USHER, CLERK *and other Officials.*

CORNWALL. Our wives will condemn him and have his life.

NORTH. Yes.

CORNWALL. I don't think we should let them have their way in too many things.

NORTH. Bodice is a good woman. But she's had to bear her troubles on her own too long. Perhaps it's too late for her to trust anyone.

CORNWALL. That's true of both of them. We'll put him in a safe prison. He'll die without us.

BODICE *and* FONTANELLE *come on. The* JUDGE *goes to them.*

BODICE. You've studied your instructions?

JUDGE. Indeed, ma'am.

BODICE. This is a political trial: politics is the higher form of justice. The old king's mad and it's dangerous to let him live. Family sentiment doesn't cloud our judgement. I've arranged to call the people who upset him most.

FONTANELLE. I'm a witness.

BODICE. Let him rattle on and condemn himself. Goad him if it helps – but not too openly.

JUDGE. I understand ma'am.

The JUDGE *takes his place.* LEAR *is brought in under guard.*

BODICE (*to* FONTANELLE). He's deteriorated. I must put the gaoler on the Honours List.

JUDGE. You are the late king?

LEAR. You know who I am. I gave you your job.

JUDGE. And these ladies are your daughters.

LEAR. No.

JUDGE. They are your daughters.

LEAR. No.

JUDGE. Don't you recognize them?

LEAR. I've never seen them.

JUDGE. Sit. (LEAR *sits*.) The late king says his daughters –

LEAR. They're not my daughters!

> BODICE *pushes* FONTANELLE. FONTANELLE *goes to the witness stand.*

FONTANELLE. I will tell the truth.

JUDGE. Ma'am, try to make the late king remember you.

FONTANELLE. Father, once you found a white horse on a battle-field. You gave it to me and it broke its leg on the ice. They tied it to a tree and shot it. Poor little Fontanelle cried.

LEAR. Poor horse.

FONTANELLE. Another time I asked you how high the wall would be. You held me over your head and said you still couldn't see over the top.

LEAR. I was always exact. – Take me back to my prison. We are freer there.

> FONTANELLE *shrugs and goes back to her seat beside* BODICE. BODICE *smiles at her. An* OLD SAILOR *is led to the witness stand.*

OLD SAILOR. I will tell the truth. I can't see. I was a sailor and the sea blinded me. I have a little sight, but in a mist. I showed you how to sail. Your voice hasn't changed. You came back when you were king and showed me your daughters. I could see in those days. These are your daughters, sir.

LEAR. Are you taken care of?

OLD SAILOR. I've been blind seven years, sir. They say I have clear eyes, but they don't see for me.

LEAR. Are you well looked after, sir?

OLD SAILOR. Yes, sir. I have a good daughter.

LEAR. Go home and watch her. They change faster than the wind at sea.

> *The* OLD SAILOR *is led away. The* OLD COUNCILLOR *goes to the witness stand.*

COUNCILLOR. I will tell the truth. (*Takes out his notebook.*) Sir, you know me.

LEAR. Through and through.

COUNCILLOR (*looks in notebook*). I helped you to escape on –

LEAR. You ran after me to be saved.

COUNCILLOR. Now you shouldn't say –

LEAR. And when you saw that I was finished you ran back here.

COUNCILLOR. I did my duty as a man of conscience –

LEAR. Convenience!

COUNCILLOR. Sir, when I saw that –

LEAR. I would be caught –

COUNCILLOR. – you were mentally disturbed –

LEAR. – you betrayed me! Is there no honour between old men? You've been corrupted by your children!

BODICE. Give him my mirror! (*Aside to* JUDGE.) Madmen are frightened of themselves!

> *The* USHER *goes towards her but* BODICE *walks past him and takes the mirror to* LEAR.

LEAR. How ugly that voice is! That's not my daughter's voice. It sounds like chains on a prison wall. (BODICE *puts the mirror in his hand and walks back to her chair.*) And she walks like something struggling in a sack. (LEAR *glances down briefly at the mirror.*) No, that's not the king.

JUDGE. Take the oath first.

LEAR. You have no right to sit there!

JUDGE. Take the oath.

LEAR. I gave you your job because you were corrupt!

JUDGE. Take the oath.

LEAR. The king is always on oath! (*He stares down at the mirror.*) No, that's not the king . . . This is a little cage of bars with an animal in it. (*Peers closer.*) No, no, that's not the king! (*Suddenly gestures violently. The* USHER *takes the mirror.*) Who shut that animal in that cage? Let it out. Have you seen its face behind the bars? There's a poor animal with blood on its head and tears running down its face. Who did that to it? Is it a bird or a horse? It's lying in the dust and its wings are broken. Who broke its wings? Who cut off its hands so that it can't shake the bars? It's pressing its snout on the glass. Who shut that animal in a glass cage? O God, there's no pity in this world. You let it lick the blood from its hair in the corner of a cage with nowhere to hide from its tormentors. No shadow, no hole! Let that animal out of its cage! (*He takes the mirror and shows it round.*) Look! Look! Have pity. Look at its claws trying to open the cage. It's dragging its broken body over the floor. You are cruel! Cruel! Look at it lying in its corner! It's shocked and cut and shaking and licking the blood on its sides. (USHER *again takes the mirror from* LEAR.) No, no! Where are they taking it now! Not out of my sight! What will they do to it? O God, give it to me! Let me hold it and stroke it and wipe its blood! (BODICE *takes the mirror from the* USHER.) No!

BODICE. I'll polish it every day and see it's not cracked.

LEAR. Then kill it. Kill it. Kill it. Don't let her torment it. I can't live with that suffering in the world.

JUDGE. See the king's madness.

LEAR. My daughters have been murdered and these monsters have taken their place! I hear all their victims cry, where is justice?

BODICE. Yes! I've locked this animal in its cage and I will not let it out!

FONTANELLE (*laughing and jumping up and down in her seat*). Look at his tears!

LEAR. Cruelty! Cruelty! See where they hauled it up by its hair!

BODICE (*to* CLERK). Get it all down!

CLERK. Ma'am.

JUDGE. The court is adjourned.

> LEAR *is taken quickly away, and the court goes.*

LEAR (*going*). Its blood's on the steps where the prisoners come!

> *The* JUDGE *goes to* BODICE *and* FONTANELLE.

JUDGE. That went better than I expected, ma'am.

BODICE. It went as I planned. There's to be a death sentence but it's not yet decided. Good day.

> *The* JUDGE *bows and goes.* BODICE *and* FONTANELLE *are alone.*

FONTANELLE. It *was* – till your husband interfered.

BODICE. And yours! Keep him on a tighter leash! Well, they must be brought to sense. Men are always obstinate, it's their form of maturity. I've bad news. My spies have found agitators and malcontents in every village. There's going to be serious fighting – civil war.

FONTANELLE. Good! If it's there let's root it out. Meet it head on. Did you know this riffraff is commanded by a woman? Called Cordelia.

BODICE (*aside*). Yes, my sister has her own spies. Power goes to her head. The head must be squeezed. As it happens, her spies are in my pay so she can never know more than I know. But from now on I shall trust her even less. If things go well her days are numbered. (*To* FONTANELLE.) Well, we'd better go and see to our husbands. This campaign needs proper preparation.

FONTANELLE. Then we can't leave it to them!

BODICE. And the army must be purged. Victory is bad for soldiers, it lowers their morale.

They go out together.

SCENE TWO

LEAR's *cell.*
Bare, empty. A stone shelf for sitting on. SOLDIERS G *and* H *bring* LEAR *in.* SOLDIER H *drops a roll of sacking on the floor.* SOLDIER G *stands by the door. They ignore* LEAR.

SOLDIER G. Not a bad way t' earn yer livin' if it weren't for the smell.
SOLDIER H. It won't last.
SOLDIER G. Nah, they'll send us up the front with the rest.
SOLDIER H. Cross laddie 'ere off.
    SOLDIER G *marks a list and the* TWO SOLDIERS *go out.*
LEAR. I must forget! I must forget!

The GHOST OF THE GRAVE DIGGER's BOY *appears. His skin and clothes are faded. There's old, dry blood on them.*

GHOST. I heard you shout.
LEAR. Are you dead?
GHOST. Yes.
LEAR. There's an animal in a cage. I must let it out or the earth will be destroyed. There'll be great fires and the water will dry up. All the people will be burned and the wind will blow their ashes into huge columns of dust and they'll go round and round the earth for ever! We must let it out! (*Calls, bangs on the wall.*) Here! Pull your chain! Here! Break it! (*There is banging from the other side of the wall.*) What? It's here! A horse!
GHOST. No. It's other prisoners.
LEAR. Help me!

GHOST. What animal is it? I've never seen it!

LEAR. Where are my daughters! They'd help me!

GHOST. I can fetch them.

LEAR. My daughters? You can fetch them here?

GHOST. Yes.

LEAR. Fetch them! Quickly! (*The* GHOST *whistles softly.*) Where are they?

GHOST. You'll see them. Wait. (*Whistles softly again.*)

> FONTANELLE'S GHOST *appears.*

LEAR. Fontanelle!

> GHOST *whistles.* BODICE'S GHOST *appears.*

Bodice!

GHOST. Let them speak first.

> *The* DAUGHTERS' GHOSTS *move slowly at first, as if they'd been asleep.*

FONTANELLE. Do my hair . . . Father comes home today.

BODICE. I must put on my dress.

FONTANELLE. O you dress so quickly! Do my hair. (BODICE *attends to her hair.*)

LEAR. My daughters!

BODICE. They're burying soldiers in the churchyard. Father's brought the coffins on carts. The palls are covered with snow. Look, one of the horses is licking its hoof.

FONTANELLE. This morning I lay in bed and watched the wind pulling the curtains. Pull, pull, pull . . . Now I can hear that terrible bell.

LEAR. Fontanelle, you're such a little girl. (*He sits on the stone shelf.*) Sit here.

FONTANELLE. No.

LEAR. On my knees. (*He sits her on his knees.*) Such a little girl.

BODICE (*listening*). Father! I must get dressed! I must get dressed. (*She struggles frantically into her dress.*)

LEAR. That's better.

FONTANELLE. Listen to the bell and the wind.

LEAR (*wets his finger and holds it in the air*). Which way is it blowing? (BODICE *gets into the dress and comes down to him. He points at her.*) Take it off!

BODICE. No.

LEAR. Take it off. Your mother's dress!

BODICE. She's dead! She gave it to me!

LEAR (*pointing*). Take it off!

BODICE. No!

LEAR. Yes, or you will always wear it! (*He pulls her to him.*) Bodice! My poor child, you might as well have worn her shroud.

> BODICE *cries against him.* BEN, *a young orderly, comes in with a small jug and plate. He sets them on the floor.*

BEN. Don't 'ang it out, grandad. They'll be round for the empties in a minute. Don't blame me if it ain't 'ow yer like it. I ain't the chef, I'm only the 'ead waiter.

> BEN *goes out. The* DAUGHTERS' GHOSTS *sit on the floor beside* LEAR *and rest their heads on his knees. He strokes their hair.*

BODICE. Where are we?

LEAR. In a prison.

BODICE. Why?

LEAR. I don't know.

BODICE. Who put us here?

LEAR. I don't know.

FONTANELLE. I'm afraid.

LEAR. Try not to be.

BODICE. Will we get out?

LEAR. Yes.

BODICE. Are you sure?

LEAR. O yes.

BODICE. If I could hope! But this prison, the pain –

LEAR. I know it will end. Everything passes, even the waste. The fools will be silent. We won't chain ourselves to the dead, or send our children to school in the graveyard. The torturers and ministers and priests will lose their office. And we'll pass each other in the street without shuddering at what we've done to each other.

BODICE. It's peaceful now.

FONTANELLE. And still.

LEAR. The animal will slip out of its cage, and lie in the fields, and run by the river, and groom itself in the sun, and sleep in its hole from night to morning.

> THREE SOLDIERS (G, H *and* I) *come in. They are methodical and quiet.*

SOLDIER H. Watch careful an' take it all in.

SOLDIER I. Corp.

SOLDIER H. Under the sack an' in the corners. (SOLDIER G *shows him how to search.*) Can yer remember it? Five times a day. Yer skip the personal.

SOLDIER I. Corp.

SOLDIER H. Less see yer try.

SOLDIER I (*searching in the corners*). When yer off?

SOLDIER G. Tmorra. Least it's out a this 'ole.

SOLDIER I. I'll stay out a the fightin' any day!

SOLDIER H. Yer don't know nothin' about it. When there's a war on yer all end up fightin'.

SOLDIER I (*finishes his search*) Corp.

SOLDIER H. So yer're ready t' mark yer list.

SOLDIER I. Corp. (*Goes to mark his list.*)

SOLDIER H. An' did yer look under the beddin'?

SOLDIER I. Corp.

SOLDIER H. Then look under the beddin'.

SOLDIER I (*looks under the bedding*). Corp.

SOLDIER H. An' now yer can mark yer list.

SOLDIER I. Corp. (*Marks his list.*)

SOLDIER H. Nignogs! . . . (*When* SOLDIER I *has finished*.) An' on t' the next one.

The THREE SOLDIERS *go out*.

BODICE. Listen. (*She stands*.)

LEAR. Where are you going?

BODICE. Mother's dead. I must serve tea. They're ringing the bell.

LEAR. Stay here.

FONTANELLE. They're waiting. There's a long line behind the coffins. They're standing so still!

LEAR. Stay here and they can't begin. We can stay here together!

GHOST. They must go! You can't stop them!

LEAR. But my mind! My mind!

The DAUGHTERS *go*.

Listen! The animal's scratching! There's blood in its mouth. The muzzle's bleeding. It's trying to dig. It's found someone! (*He falls unconscious on his sack*.)

An OLD ORDERLY *comes in*.

OLD ORDERLY. Sing away, I won't 'urt you. I come for the plate. (*He sees it's untouched*.) O. Shall I come back? Writin' petitions an' appeals an' retainin' yer self respect an' keepin' yer mind occupied – thass all right, but yer must eat. Well, yer know yer own stomach. (*Reassuringly*.) I ain' on the staff. (*Slight pause*.) They're sendin' the young filth up the front. Let 'em rot. Waste a good bullets. I come in 'ere thousands a years back, 'undreds a thousands. I don't know what I come in for. I forgot. I 'eard so many tell what they come in for it's all mixed up in me 'ead. I've 'eard every crime in the book confessed t' me. Must be a record. Don't know which was mine now. Murder? Robbin'? Violence? I'd like t' know. Juss t' put me mind t' rest. Satisfy me conscience. But no one knows now. It's all gone. Long ago. The records is lost. 'Undreds a years back. (*Points to plate.*) Shall I wait? (*No answer.*) The customer knows what 'e wants.

The OLD ORDERLY *takes the plate and mug and goes out.*

LEAR. I shouldn't have looked. I killed so many people and never looked at one of their faces. But I looked at that animal. Wrong. Wrong. Wrong. It's made me a stupid old man. What colour's my hair?

GHOST. White.

LEAR. I'm frightened to look. There's blood on it where I pulled it with these hands.

GHOST. Let me stay with you, Lear. When I died I went somewhere. I don't know where it was. I waited and nothing happened. And then I started to rot, like a body in the ground. Look at my hands, they're like an old man's. They're withered. I'm young but my stomach's shrivelled up and the hair's turned white. Look, my arms! Feel how thin I am. (LEAR *doesn't move.*) Are you afraid to touch me?

LEAR. No.

GHOST. Feel.

LEAR (*hesitates. Feels*). Yes, thin.

GHOST. I'm afraid. Let me stay with you, keep me here, please.

LEAR. Yes, yes, Poor boy. Lie down by me. Here. I'll hold you. We'll help each other. Cry while I sleep, and I'll cry and watch you while you sleep. We'll take turns. The sound of the human voice will comfort us.

SCENE THREE

Rebel field post.
CORDELIA *and some* REBEL SOLDIERS. PETE *nurses a* WOUNDED REBEL SOLDIER *called* TERRY. LEWIS *stands upstage as look-out.*
SOLDIER I *sits with his hands tied behind his back and no cap. Beside him is a* CROUCHING REBEL SOLDIER *with a rifle. Some of*

the other REBEL SOLDIERS *carry rifles. They wear simple, utilitarian clothes, not uniforms. There is a tense silence.*

LEWIS (*looks off*). They're coming.

CORDELIA (*relaxes a little and goes to the* WOUNDED REBEL SOLDIER). Is he all right?

PETE. There's no drugs, no equipment, nothing.

The CARPENTER *comes on with two more* REBEL SOLDIERS. *They carry rifles and bundles.*

CARPENTER. What was the firing?

CORDELIA. Some scouts found us. It's all right, we got them. What did you bring?

CARPENTER. Tea, spuds, two blankets. They won't take money. They want to join us.

CORDELIA. How many?

CARPENTER. Up to twenty.

CORDELIA. Will they bring their own supplies?

CARPENTER. Yes.

CORDELIA. We'll pick them up when we move through. We're almost ready.

CARPENTER (*indicates* SOLDIER I). One of the scouts?

CORDELIA. Yes. The rest were shot. I wanted to talk to him first. Terry was hit.

CARPENTER. O . . .

The two REBEL SOLDIERS *who have just arrived drink tea quickly. The other* REBEL SOLDIERS *carry their bundles offstage. A* REBEL SOLDIER *hands a mug of tea to the* CARPENTER.

CORDELIA (*to* SOLDIER I). How far did you come?

SOLDIER I. 'Ard t' say. We never come straight an' the maps is US. I was born in the city. These fields are China t' me.

CORDELIA. How long did you march?

SOLDIER I. O I can tell yer that. We moved off at first light.

CARPENTER (*sips his tea*). They've reached the river.

SOLDIER I. Yeh, we come over a river. On, a rope – that was a giggle. The farmers'd burned the real bridge. My life!

CORDELIA. What are your supplies like?

SOLDIER I. Nothin'. They used t' be regular. Now everythin's burned. We come through this town. Same thing – burned. Nothin' t' loot. A nice place once.

CORDELIA. Why d'you fight us?

SOLDIER I. I'm more afraid a me own lot than I am a yourn. I'd make a run for it but I'd get a bullet in me back. Not that I'm knockin' your lads! After all, I'm one a you if yer like t' look at it. If I lived out in the sticks I'd be fightin' with you lot, wouldn't I?

> CORDELIA *and the* CARPENTER *walk away.*

CARPENTER. Let him join us.

CORDELIA. He's a child, he crawls where he's put down. He'd talk to anyone who caught him. To fight like us you must hate, we can't trust a man unless he hates. Otherwise he has no use. (*To* CROUCHING REBEL SOLDIER.) We've finished.

> CROUCHING REBEL SOLDIER *and* LEWIS *start to take* SOLDIER I *out. Another* SOLDIER *takes* LEWIS's *place as look-out.*

SOLDIER I. 'Ello, we goin' then?

> *The three go out.* CARPENTER *looks at the* WOUNDED REBEL SOLDIER.

CARPENTER. Where?

PETE. Stomach.

WOUNDED SOLDIER. It's all right, don't whisper. I won't be a nuisance. We said we'd die quietly, if we could. Don't scream or ask for anything. It upsets the others and holds them up . . .

CORDELIA. You must rest before we –

WOUNDED SOLDIER. Yes, yes. Don't treat me like a child because I'm dying. Let me drink some water.

PETE. No.

WOUNDED SOLDIER. It doesn't matter about my stomach. It'll help my throat. (CARPENTER *gives him some water*.) Yes. Now go and get ready.

They leave him and get ready to move.

CORDELIA (*to the* LOOK-OUT). Tell them to start moving. Keep off the road.

The LOOK-OUT *goes out.*

WOUNDED SOLDIER. When it's dark I'll pretend my wife's come to meet me and they're coming up the road. I put our girl on my shoulder and she pulls my hair and I say ah . . .

PETE. More tea?

CARPENTER. No.

PETE *empties the tea can and packs it.*

WOUNDED SOLDIER. She sees a bird and asks me what it is and I say it's a wader but I don't know . . . Who'll tell my wife I'm dead?

Off, a single shot. No one reacts.

It's dark, there are the stars . . . look . . .

LEWIS *and the* CROUCHING SOLDIER *come back. They pick up their things.*

CORDELIA. When we have power these things won't be necessary.

Everyone goes off except the WOUNDED SOLDIER.

WOUNDED SOLDIER. The stars . . . Look . . . One . . . Two . . . Three . . .

Silence.

SCENE FOUR

HQ.

BODICE *sleeps slumped forward over a desk. On the desk a map, documents, pen, ink, teacher's bell. By the desk,* BODICE's *knitting bag full of documents. Off, a knock.* BODICE *hears and moves but doesn't sit up. Off, a second knock.* BODICE *sits up and rings the bell once. An* AIDE *comes in.*

AIDE. Your sister's here now, ma'am.

BODICE. What time is it?

AIDE. Two.

BODICE. Let her in.

> AIDE *lets* FONTANELLE *in and goes out.*

FONTANELLE. Your aide says our husbands have run away!

BODICE. They met the Chiefs of Staff this afternoon. The army thinks we'll lose the war.

FONTANELLE. Impossible. We're fighting peasants.

BODICE. The army thinks –

FONTANELLE. They can't think! Our husbands ran our campaign, that's why we lost. But if they're gone now, we'll win!

BODICE. You silly woman, haven't you learned anything yet? I had to send troops to bring them back. They're downstairs now.

FONTANELLE. Why?

BODICE. Why? We need their armies!

FONTANELLE. O – they'll fight for us!

BODICE. They wouldn't break a grasshopper's leg for us. Why d'you think I put up with my husband for so long?

FONTANELLE. Put up with him?

BODICE. O don't waste your hypocrisy on me. You tried to kill yours once. My spies told me and they don't lie. They're the only moral institution in this country.

FONTANELLE (*shrugs*). Well, I don't bother any more. He's stopped slobbering over me and I sleep with whom I like.

BODICE. It must be getting difficult to find someone.

FONTANELLE (*after a pause, in a small voice*). Well I don't wake them up in the middle of the night to ask them to hold my wool. Is that why you sleep alone?

BODICE. At least they'd get to sleep first. Sign these before you go.

FONTANELLE. What are they?

BODICE. Various warrants. We'll have to run the country between us – but you're no good at office work, it's a waste of time you trying.

FONTANELLE. I'll only sign what doesn't conflict with my conscience. (*Picks up a document.*) What's this?

BODICE. Father's death warrant.

FONTANELLE. Where's the pen?

BODICE (*as* FONTANELLE *signs*). There are a number of old matters it's politically dangerous to leave open. They should have been closed long ago, but it's been left to us, of course!

FONTANELLE. Where is he?

BODICE. They're bringing a batch of prisoners to HQ. They had to evacuate the prisons. The warrants will be carried out when they arrive. Sign the others.

A signal is tapped on the door. BODICE *rings the bell once.* TWO PLAINCLOTHES SPIES *bring the* DUKES OF CORNWALL *and* NORTH *in. They have been questioned but not marked. Their jackets, belts and laces have been removed. They look flushed.* BODICE *stands.*

No – be silent! Not one word! There's nothing to explain. My spies have learned more about you than you know yourselves, and none of it came as a surprise to me.

FONTANELLE. Burn them!

BODICE. Be quiet! You will be kept in cells until we need you to be seen in public, or for any other reason. (NORTH *opens his mouth to speak.*) Be quiet! While you are out of your cells you will at all times be accompanied by my plainclothes spies. If you misbehave in any way you will be instantly shot. (NORTH

opens his mouth to speak.) Will you be quiet! – We would explain
it away as an assassination by the enemy.

FONTANELLE. Burn them! I'm superstitious, they'll bring us bad
luck.

BODICE. Take them downstairs.

> The TWO PLAINCLOTHES SPIES *take the* DUKES OF NORTH
> *and* CORNWALL *out.*

FONTANELLE. And what will you do about the war?

BODICE (*rings the bell once*). You'd better go back to bed. You
mustn't keep your chauffeur waiting.

> FONTANELLE *goes towards the door and meets the* AIDE
> *coming in.*

FONTANELLE. Major Pellet, don't let my sister overwork you.

AIDE. We're very busy, ma'am.

FONTANELLE. If she bullies you let me know.

AIDE. Ma'am.

> FONTANELLE *goes out.* BODICE *hands him the warrants.*

BODICE. Hand these to the adjutant. Morning will do.

AIDE. Yes, ma'am.

> The AIDE *goes out.* BODICE *looks at the map.*

BODICE. War. Power. (*Off,* FONTANELLE *laughs briefly, and then
the* AIDE *laughs briefly.*) I'm forced to sit at this desk, work with
my sister, walk beside my husband. They say decide this and
that, but I don't decide anything. My decisions are forced on
me. I change people's lives and things get done – it's like a
mountain moving forward, but not because I tell it to. I started
to pull the wall down, and I had to stop that – the men are
needed here. (*She taps the map with the finger tips of one hand.*)
And now I must move them here and here – (*She moves her
index finger on the map.*) – because the map's my straitjacket and
that's all I can do. I'm trapped. (*Off, a clock strikes rapidly.
Silence. She thinks about her life, but not reflectively. She is*

trying to understand what has happened to her.) I hated being a girl, but at least I was happy sometimes. And it was better when I grew up, I could be myself – they didn't humiliate me then. I was almost free! I made so many plans, one day I'd be my own master! Now I have all the power . . . and I'm a slave. Worse! (*Rings the bell once.*) Pellet! – I shall work. I shall pounce on every mistake my enemy makes! (*Rings the bell once.*) War is so full of chances! I only need a little luck. (*Rings the bell twice.*) Pellet! Pellet! (*Picks up the map and starts to go.*) Are you asleep?

    She goes out.

SCENE FIVE

Road.
Prison convoy on a country road. LEAR *and* FOUR PRISONERS *chained together by the neck and blindfolded.* LEAR *is also gagged. They are led and guarded by* THREE SOLDIERS (J, K *and* L). *Everyone is tired and dirty. They talk nervously and quietly, all except* LEAR. *Continuous heavy gun fire in the distance.*

SOLDIER J (*looking at a map*). Useless bloody map!

SOLDIER K (*looks round*). We're lost!

SOLDIER J. Shut up! (*To* PRISONERS.) Hup hup!

FIRST PRISONER (*quietly*). Can't go anymore.

SECOND PRISONER. Lean on me.

SOLDIER K. Hup.

THIRD PRISONER (*to* SECOND PRISONER). Let 'im go. 'E knows when e's 'ad enough.

SOLDIER L. Hup.

SECOND PRISONER. No. They'll shoot him.

SOLDIER K. We're 'eadin' back the way we come.

SOLDIER J. 'Alt! (*The* PRISONERS *stop immediately.*) Down. (*They sit. To* SOLDIER K.) Go 'an 'ave a little reccy. You're good at directions.

SOLDIER K *goes out. The* PRISONERS *pass round a water can. They don't remove their blindfolds.*

FOURTH PRISONER. I'm next.

SOLDIER J (*crouches and studies map*). They must a issued this for the Crimea.

SECOND PRISONER (*gives water to* FIRST PRISONER). I'll hold it.

SOLDIER L. I tol' yer t' wrap it.

SOLDIER J. Wha' direction's the firin' comin' from?

SOLDIER L. Moves about.

SECOND PRISONER. Enough.

FIRST PRISONER. Thank you.

SECOND PRISONER. I'll try to look where we are. Keep in front of me.

FOURTH PRISONER. Here. (*The water can is passed to him. It's almost empty.*) Bastards! It's empty! (*Drinks.*)

THIRD PRISONER. Leave some. (*Takes the water can.*)

SOLDIER L (*sees* SECOND PRISONER *trying to look*). Oi wass your game!

SOLDIER J. Wass up?

SECOND PRISONER. Nothing. Nothing.

SOLDIER L. I saw yer look.

SECOND PRISONER. No.

SOLDIER J. 'E look?

SOLDIER L. Yeh! Any more out a you and yer'll look through a 'ole in yer 'ead. I got the enemy breathin' up me arse. I ain' messin' about with you, sonny.

The TWO SOLDIERS *go back to the map.*

SOLDIER J (*looking off*). Wass keepin' 'im?

SOLDIER L. Don't tell me 'e's gone an' got lost now. Why don't we run for it?

SOLDIER J (*indicates* PRISONERS). What about these darlin's?

SOLDIER L. Leave 'em, kill 'em.

SOLDIER J. Give it another minute. Best t' stick t' orders as long as yer can.

SOLDIER L (*grumbling nastily*). I ain' cartin' this garbage round much longer, we ain' safe ourselves. (*Suddenly calls after* SOLDIER K, *low and intense.*) Billy? (*Silence.*) 'E don't 'ear. Reckon 'e's scarpered?

SOLDIER J. Billy? Nah.

THIRD PRISONER (*removes gag from* LEAR'*s mouth and holds the water can against it*). 'Ere, drink this an' be quiet.

LEAR (*after drinking a mouthful*). More.

FOURTH PRISONER. It's gone.

LEAR. I can't see.

THIRD PRISONER. Our eyes are covered.

LEAR. Where are we?

SOLDIER L. Joker. 'Oo unplugged 'is gob?

LEAR (*loudly and serenely*). Why do they pull me about like this? Why do they waste their time on me. If they let me I'd go away quietly. How could I harm them? They're young, why do they waste their life leading an old man on a rope?

The distant guns sound louder.

SOLDIER L. 'Ark at it! (*Calls as before.*) Billy?

SOLDIER J. Leave it.

SOLDIER L. I'll go an' look for 'im.

SOLDIER J. O no you don't.

LEAR. I've lost my boy.

SOLDIER L (*to* PRISONERS). I ain' warnin' yer. Keep 'im quiet.

LEAR. There are so many voices! I must find him. I had a terrible pain in my head and he stopped it and now I must help him. He's lost. He needs me. What will they do to him if I'm not there to call them off? Boy! Boy! Hey!

SOLDIER L. All right, bloody 'ush!

LEAR (*stands*). Here! Here!

FOURTH PRISONER. Stop him! My neck!

SOLDIER J. E's bloody mad!

FOURTH PRISONER. Kick him!

SOLDIER L (*runs to* LEAR *and gags him*). I said stow it, grandad. Now bloody talk t' yerself. (*He goes back to* SOLDIER J, *who is still by the map.*) Get yer rifle. They've 'ad long enough.

SOLDIER J. Give 'em a little bit longer. (*He kneels in front of the map.*) We must be on 'ere somewhere.

> *Pause.* LEAR *makes sounds through his gag. Slowly* SOLDIERS J *and* L *raise their hands over their heads – they look like Moslems about to pray.* SOLDIER K *comes on with his hands above his head. They stay like this in silence for a few moments. The* CARPENTER, LEWIS, PETE *and other* REBEL SOLDIERS *come on. They are quick, quiet and tense.*

CARPENTER. This them?

SOLDIER K. Yeh.

> LEWIS *goes upstage as Look Out. A* REBEL SOLDIER *picks up* SOLDIERS J *and* L's *rifles.*

CARPENTER. Anyone in charge?

SOLDIER J. 'Ere.

CARPENTER. Where were you wanting to get to?

SOLDIER J. HQ. Evacuating that lot.

CARPENTER. You haven't got an HQ left.

FOURTH PRISONER (*takes off his blindfold*). We're free . . . (*The* PRISONERS *hesitate awkwardly.*) Can we take the chains off?

CARPENTER. No. Not till the political officers have been through you. (*Points to* SOLDIERS J, K *and* L.) Tie them up.

> *The* THREE SOLDIER'*s hands are tied behind their backs. The* CARPENTER *goes to the side of the stage, whistles, and gestures to someone to come on.*

FOURTH PRISONER. You can undo me. I'm a political prisoner. On your side. I shall have influence when things are changed. I'll put in a word for you soldiers. You've saved my life.

FONTANELLE *and a* REBEL SOLDIER *come on from the direction of the* CARPENTER'S *whistle. Her hands are tied behind her back. She is dirty and dishevelled and her clothes are torn.*

CARPENTER. Tie her on the end.

PETE (*tying* FONTANELLE *on to the chain of* PRISONERS). Can they take their blindfolds off?

CARPENTER. If you like.

The PRISONERS *remove their blindfolds.* THIRD PRISONER *takes* LEAR'S *off.*

LEAR. Undo this chain. My hands are white. There's no blood in them. My neck's like old leather. You'd have a job to hang me now. I don't want to live except for the boy. Who'd look after him?

FONTANELLE. Don't tie me up with him! (*Cries with anger.*) O God, how foul . . .

LEAR. Who's crying? (*Still serenely. He doesn't recognize her.*) Stop that, child. Ask them quietly. You're a woman, you should know how to do that. Some of them are kind, some of them listen.

FONTANELLE. You stupid, stupid, wicked fool!

LEAR. You mustn't shout. No one will listen to that. They all shout here.

CARPENTER. Who is he? I've seen him before.

SOLDIER J. Don't know any of 'em from Adam. That one thinks 'e's king.

CARPENTER. It'd be safer to be Jesus Christ.

Off, a whistle.

LEWIS. We're off. (*He whistles back.*)

PETE. On your feet. (*The* PRISONERS *stand.*)

FONTANELLE. Don't take me like this. The people will throw stones at me and shout. They hate me. I'm afraid. I'll faint and

scream. I've never been humiliated, I don't know how to
behave. Help me. Please.

LEAR. Don't ask them for favours. Walk with us. Be gentle and
don't pull.

CARPENTER. Watch that old one. He's a trouble maker.

LEAR. We'll go decently and quietly and look for my boy. He was
very good to me. He saved my mind when I went mad. And to
tell you the truth I did him a great wrong once, a very great
wrong. He's never blamed me. I must be kind to him now.
Come on, we'll find him together.

> *They go out in the direction from which the* PRISONERS *came
> on.*

SCENE SIX

LEAR's *cell.*
It is darker than before. LEAR, FONTANELLE *and the* PRISONERS
from the chain gang (except FOURTH PRISONER) *are sitting on the
ground. A bare electric bulb hangs from the ceiling. It is unlit. Off, a
sudden burst of rifle shots.*

FIRST PRISONER (*jumps up*). They're starting again!

SECOND PRISONER. No. They said last week it was only once.
They got rid of the undesirables then. (*Trying to sound calm.*)
We mustn't panic.

> *The* OLD ORDERLY *comes on with a bucket and puts it down
> upstage.*

THIRD PRISONER. Yeh, they're still feedin' us. They wouldn't
waste grub . . .

SECOND PRISONER (*to* OLD ORDERLY). What are they doing?

OLD ORDERLY. Never noticed.

FIRST PRISONER. We heard shooting.

OLD ORDERLY. Could 'ave. My 'earin' went 'undred a years back.

THIRD PRISONER. Why are they keepin' us 'ere? We should a bin out by now.

OLD ORDERLY. No orders, no papers, no forms, nothing comes through – no one knows what to do.

The OLD ORDERLY *goes out. Everyone eats except* LEAR *and* FIRST PRISONER. *They watch each other hungrily while they eat.* FONTANELLE *only eats a little.* LEAR *sits on the ground. He is still calm and remote.*

SECOND PRISONER (*jostling at the bucket*). Steady!

The GRAVEDIGGER'S BOY'S GHOST *comes on. He is white and thin.*

LEAR. Where have you been? Are you in pain?

GHOST. What? I don't know. I'm so cold. See how thin I am. Look at my legs. I think my chest's empty inside. Where have you been?

LEAR. Some men took us out of the town and along a road and some more men stopped us and brought us back again. I was lonely without you and worried, but I knew I'd find you. (LEAR *and the* GHOST *sit and lean against each other.*)

GHOST. Tell me what you saw. This city's like a grave. I tried to follow you but when we got out in the open the wind was too strong, it pushed me back.

LEAR. There was so much sky. I could hardly see. I've always looked down at the hills and banks where the enemy was hiding. But there's only a little strip of earth and all the sky. You're like my son now. I wish I'd been your father. I'd have looked after you so well.

The COMMANDANT, OLD ORDERLY *and* THREE SOLDIERS (M, N *and* O) *come in. The* SOLDIERS *carry rifles.*

COMMANDANT. What's that food bucket doing here?

OLD ORDERLY. They're always fed at this time. It's on standin'
  orders.

COMMANDANT. You old fool. (*Reads from a list.*) Evans.

THIRD PRISONER. Yeh.

COMMANDANT. M413. Leave that. L37 Hewit.

SECOND PRISONER. Yes.

COMMANDANT. H257 Wellstone.

FIRST PRISONER. Yes.

COMMANDANT. Outside.

SOLDIER M. Get fell in sharp.

SECOND PRISONER. We're on the wrong list.

SOLDIER N. Tell me that outside.

THIRD PRISONER. We're politicals.

SECOND PRISONER. I was on your side. That's why I'm here.

COMMANDANT. It's all been cleared up. You're transferees. Outside, there's good lads.

SECOND PRISONER. No.

> SOLDIERS M *and* N *run* SECOND PRISONER *out. He shouts
> 'No!' once more before he goes.* COMMANDANT *and* SOLDIER
> O *take* FIRST *and* THIRD PRISONERS *outside. The* OLD
> ORDERLY *picks up some scraps of food from the floor and drops
> them in the bucket.* LEAR *goes to the bucket to feed.*

OLD ORDERLY. Throw their muck anywhere.

FONTANELLE. For as long as I can remember there was misery
  and waste and suffering wherever you were. You live in your
  own mad world, you can't hear me. You've wasted my life and
  I can't even tell you. O God, where can I find justice?

LEAR. They didn't leave much.

> *Off, a burst of rifle shots.*

OLD ORDERLY. Do this, run there, fetch that, carry this. Finished?
  (*He picks up the bucket.*) No one can put a foot right today. Job
  like this upsets the whole place. (*Starts to go.*) Work. Work.
  Work.

The OLD ORDERLY *goes out.* FONTANELLE *goes to* LEAR.

FONTANELLE. Talk to them! Say you know something the government ought to know. Promise them something. Anything. Make them – negotiate! – put us on trial! O father, you must think!

LEAR. He's taken the bucket. I always scrape it.

FONTANELLE. Bodice is still fighting. She'll beat them, she always does. Help me, father. If Bodice saves us I'll look after you. I understand you now. Take everything back. God knows I don't want it. Look, let me help you. Father, think. Try. Talk to them, argue with them – you're so good at that. Sit down. (*She brushes hair from his face.*) We mustn't shout at each other. I do love you. I'm such a stupid woman. Yes (*She laughs.*) – stupid, stupid! But you understand me. What will you say to them?

LEAR. All the sky.

FONTANELLE. Remember! Remember!

LEAR. And a little piece of earth.

The CARPENTER, COMMANDANT, OLD ORDERLY, FOURTH PRISONER *and* SOLDIERS M, N *and* O *come in.* FOURTH PRISONER *wears a crumpled, dark-blue striped suit.*

COMMANDANT (*to* SOLDIERS, *indicating the cell*). Keep this one separate for the family.

FONTANELLE. Are you putting us on trial?

CARPENTER. Your father's case is still open. But yours has been closed.

FONTANELLE (*calmer*). If I appealed it would go to you?

CARPENTER. Yes.

FONTANELLE. My sister will punish you if you do anything to us!

CARPENTER. We've got her. We're bringing her here.

Off, a burst of rifle shots.

FONTANELLE (*agitated again*). Let me swallow poison. You don't

care how I die as long as you get rid of me. Why must you hurt
me?

CARPENTER (*shakes his head*). No. I can't stay long and I must see
it finished. I have to identify the body.

> SOLDIER N *shoots* FONTANELLE *from behind. She falls dead
> immediately.*

COMMANDANT. Will you wait in my office? It's warmer.

CARPENTER. Thank you.

> *The* COMMANDANT *and* CARPENTER *go out wearily.*
> SOLDIERS M *and* N *follow them.* LEAR, GHOST, FOURTH
> PRISONER *and* SOLDIER O *are left.* SOLDIER O *helps* FOURTH
> PRISONER *to erect a trestle table.*

FOURTH PRISONER. Bring this here.

> SOLDIER O *helps* FOURTH PRISONER *to put* FONTA-
> NELLE'*s body on the table. They move quietly and efficiently.*
> FOURTH PRISONER *switches on the bare electric light over the
> table. He has turned his white shirt-cuffs back over his jacket
> sleeves. The* GHOST *cringes away.* LEAR *stares at* FOURTH
> PRISONER. *Slowly he stands. He begins to see where he is.*

GHOST. It's beginning.

LEAR. What?

GHOST. Quickly, Lear! I'll take you away! We'll go to the place
where I was lost!

LEAR. No. I ran away so often, but my life was ruined just the
same. Now I'll stay. (*He stares at* FOURTH PRISONER.)

FOURTH PRISONER (*efficiently*). I'm the prison medical doctor.
We met in less happy times. I said I was in good standing with
the government. My papers confirmed that. I'm just waiting for
more papers and then I'll be given a post of more obvious trust
and importance. We're ready to begin.

LEAR. What are you doing?

FOURTH PRISONER. A little autopsy. Not a big one. We know
what she died of. But I handle this routine work methodically.

Otherwise they think you can't be trusted with bigger things. My new papers will open up many new opportunities for me.

LEAR. Who was she?

FOURTH PRISONER. Your daughter.

LEAR. Did I have a daughter?

FOURTH PRISONER. Yes, it's on her chart. That's her stomach and the liver underneath. I'm just making a few incisions to satisfy the authorities.

LEAR. Is that my daughter . . .? (*Points.*) That's . . .?

FOURTH PRISONER. The stomach.

LEAR (*points*). That?

FOURTH PRISONER. The lungs. You can see how she died. The bullet track goes through the lady's lungs.

LEAR. But where is the . . . She was cruel and angry and hard . . .

FOURTH PRISONER (*points*). The womb.

LEAR. So much blood and bits and pieces packed in with all that care. Where is the . . . where . . .?

FOURTH PRISONER. What is the question?

LEAR. Where is the beast? The blood is as still as a lake. Where . . .? Where . . .?

FOURTH PRISONER (*to* SOLDIER O). What's the man asking? (*No response.*)

LEAR. She sleeps inside like a lion and a lamb and a child. The things are so beautiful. I am astonished. I have never seen anything so beautiful. If I had known she was so beautiful . . . Her body was made by the hand of a child, so sure and nothing unclean . . . If I had known this beauty and patience and care, how I would have loved her.

The GHOST *starts to cry but remains perfectly still.*

Did I make this – and destroy it?

BODICE *is brought in by* SOLDIERS M *and* N. *She is dirty and dishevelled, but she has tried to clean herself and tidy her hair. She tries to sound eager and in control.*

BODICE. In here? Yes. Thank you. Did my letter go to the
government?

SOLDIER M. Wait 'ere.

BODICE. Yes. Thank you. I must see someone in authority. I
want to explain my letter, you see. (*Sees* LEAR.) O, yes, they've
put us together. That must be a friendly sign. Now I know they
mean to act properly!

FOURTH PRISONER. Pass me my forms. (SOLDIER O *hands him
some forms.*)

BODICE (*brightly trying to show interest*). What are you doing?

LEAR. That's your sister.

BODICE. No!

LEAR. I destroyed her.

BODICE. Destroyed? No, no! We admit nothing. We acted for
the best. Did what we had to do.

LEAR. I destroyed her! I knew nothing, saw nothing, learned
nothing! Fool! Fool! Worse than I knew! (*He puts his hands into*
FONTANELLE *and brings them out with organs and viscera. The*
SOLDIERS *react awkwardly and ineffectually.*) Look at my dead
daughter!

BODICE. No! No!

LEAR. Look! I killed her! Her blood is on my hands! Destroyer!
Murderer! And now I must begin again. I must walk through
my life, step after step, I must walk in weariness and bitterness,
I must become a child, hungry and stripped and shivering in
blood, I must open my eyes and see!

> The COMMANDANT *runs in shouting and pointing at the*
> SOLDIERS.

COMMANDANT. You! – You! – What is this? Get it under
control!

FOURTH PRISONER. I tried to stop them – saboteurs! – don't let
this stop my petition –

> The CARPENTER *comes in.*

BODICE. Thank God! At last! I wrote to your wife. She's sent you to me. She accepts my offer to collaborate. I was against the fighting. I can show you minutes. My father's mad, you can see that – and my sister drove him on!

CARPENTER. The government found no extenuating circumstances in your case.

BODICE. O – but you haven't been told everything. You must acquaint yourself with the facts. No, I don't expect you to let me go. I'm culpable by association. I've been foolish. I accept that. Now there must be a term of imprisonment. I fully accept it.

CARPENTER. You were sentenced to death.

BODICE. No! You have no right! I will not be dealt with by your – committee! I have a right to justice in court! O you are cruel when you get a little power – when you have the power I had you beg people to accept your mercy so that God will not judge you! (*Falls down.*) Please. Please. Please.

CARPENTER. Be quick.

> SOLDIER N *moves behind* BODICE *with a pistol. She sees him and fights furiously.* SOLDIER M *and* O *join in. They can't see to aim.* SOLDIER O *fixes a bayonet.* BODICE *bites* SOLDIER M.

SOLDIER M. Bitch!

> SOLDIER M *throws her to the ground again. She writhes away and screams.*

'Old 'er still!

> SOLDIER N *kicks her.* SOLDIERS M *and* N *pinion her with their boots. She writhes and screams.*

'Old 'er! 'Old 'er!

> SOLDIER O *bayonets her three times. Slight pause. She writhes. He bayonets her once again. She gives a spasm and dies.*

CARPENTER. Thank you. I'm sorry. You're good lads.
SOLDIER O. . . . . Blimey.
COMMANDANT (*to* SOLDIERS). Clear up, lads.

> The CARPENTER *starts to go. The* COMMANDANT *stops him.*
> *While the* COMMANDANT *and the* CARPENTER *talk,* SOL-
> DIERS *remove* FONTANELLE, BODICE *and the trestle table*
> *and turn off the light.*
> (*He tries to force the* CARPENTER.)

We should finish everything. There's still the old man.
CARPENTER. You know I can't. My wife says no. She knew him.
COMMANDANT. I've been having a word with the prison MO.
  Very reliable man, sir. (*He beckons* FOURTH PRISONER *over.*)
  About the old one.
FOURTH PRISONER. If he has to be kept alive –
CARPENTER. I've already explained that –
FOURTH PRISONER. I follow, sir. Then he could be made
  politically ineffective.
CARPENTER. What does that mean?
FOURTH PRISONER. Madmen often harm themselves.
CARPENTER. But not killed. That's too obvious.
FOURTH PRISONER. Only harmed.
CARPENTER. Well, anything happens in a war.
COMMANDANT. Good.

> The COMMANDANT *and* CARPENTER *go out.*

FOURTH PRISONER. This is a chance to bring myself to notice.

> FOURTH PRISONER *goes upstage into the dark.*

SOLDIER M. She bit me. What yer do for snake bite?
SOLDIER N (*looks*). I'd burn that.
SOLDIER O. Thass only a dose a rabbies.

> FOURTH PRISONER *comes downstage with a heap of equipment.*
> *The* GHOST *stands and watches silently.* LEAR *is immobile.*
> *He is completely withdrawn.*

FOURTH PRISONER. Right. (*He goes to* LEAR.) Good morning. Time for your drive. Into your coat. (LEAR *is put into a strait-jacket. He doesn't help in any way.*) Cross your arms and hold your regalia. Now the buttons. This nasty wind gets in everywhere. You've been inside too long to trust yourself to fresh air. (LEAR *is seated on a chair.*) Get settled down. (*His legs are strapped to the chair legs.*) And last your crown. (*A square frame is lowered over his head and face.* FOURTH PRISONER *steps back. Then* LEAR *speaks.*)

LEAR. You've turned me into a king again.

FOURTH PRISONER (*produces a tool*). Here's a device I perfected on dogs for removing human eyes.

LEAR. No, no. You mustn't touch my eyes. I must have my eyes!

FOURTH PRISONER. With this device you extract the eye undamaged and then it can be put to good use. It's based on a scouting gadget I had as a boy.

SOLDIER N. Get on. It's late.

FOURTH PRISONER. Understand, this isn't an instrument of torture, but a scientific device. See how it clips the lid back to leave it unmarked.

LEAR. No – no!

FOURTH PRISONER. Nice and steady. (*He removes one of* LEAR'*s eyes.*)

LEAR. Aahh!

FOURTH PRISONER. Note how the eye passes into the lower chamber and is received into a soothing solution of formaldehyde crystals. One more, please. (*He removes* LEAR'*s other eye.*)

LEAR. Aaahhh!

FOURTH PRISONER (*looking at the eyes in the glass container*). Perfect.

LEAR (*jerking in the chair*). Aaahhh! The sun! It hurts my eyes!

FOURTH PRISONER (*sprays an aerosol into* LEAR'*s eye sockets*). That will assist the formation of scab and discourage flies. (*To* SOLDIERS.) Clean this up with a bucket and mop.

FOURTH PRISONER *starts to leave.*

LEAR. Aaahhh! It hurts!

FOURTH PRISONER. Keep still. You make it worse.

FOURTH PRISONER *goes out.*

SOLDIER M. Less get away an' shut the door.

SOLDIER N. 'E'll 'ave the 'ole bloody place up.

SOLDIER O. O lor.

The THREE SOLDIERS *go out.* LEAR *and the* GHOST *are left.*

LEAR. Aaahhh! The roaring in my head. I see blood. (*Spits.*) Blood in my mouth. (*Jerks.*) My hands – undo my hands and let me kill myself.

GHOST. Lear.

LEAR. Who's that! What d'you want? You can't take my eyes, but take the rest! Kill me! Kill me!

GHOST. No – people will be kind to you now. Surely you've suffered enough.

LEAR. You. (*The* GHOST *starts to unfasten* LEAR.) Tell me the pain will stop! This pain must stop! O stop, stop, stop!

GHOST. It will stop. Sometimes it might come back, but you'll learn to bear it. I can stay with you now you need me.

LEAR. Wipe my mouth. There's blood. I'm swallowing blood.

GHOST. Stand. Please. (LEAR *stumbles to his feet.*) Walk as if you could see. Try. We'll go back to my house. It's quiet there, they'll leave you in peace at last.

LEAR (*stumbling forward*). Take me away! This pain must stop! Ah! (*Stumbling out.*) Take me somewhere to die!

LEAR *stumbles out with the* GHOST.

SCENE SEVEN

Near the wall.
Open fields.
A FARMER, *his* WIFE *and* SON *hurry on. They cross upstage. They
carry bundles.*

SON. Doo come. Thass late.

FARMER'S WIFE. Don't fret. Goo on, we'll keep up.

    LEAR *stumbles on downstage with the* GHOST. LEAR *now carries
    a stick.*

LEAR. Where are we, where are we? The wind's stinging my eyes.
They're full of dust.

GHOST. We're near the wall. It'll be easier to walk along the top.
Stop. There's some people here. Shall we hide in the scrub?

LEAR. No. I must beg.

    LEAR *takes out a bowl and begs.*

Alms! I'm not a criminal, I wasn't blinded by a judge. Alms!

    The FARMER, *his* WIFE *and* SON *come down to* LEAR.

FARMER. Good day, father. (*He looks at the bowl. His* SON *makes a
gesture of refusal.*) We ont got no bait for yoo. We're poor people
off the land. Thass my wife an' my littl' ol' boy by me here.

LEAR. Can I rest in your house? I'm so tired.

FARMER. Yoo'd be welcome an' more, but thass gone. See, sir,
when the ol' king went mad they stop buildin' his wall, an' a
great crowd a people come up these parts. The ol' king cleared
a good strip a land both sides his wall. Rare land that was. So we
took a plow an' built ourselves homes.

FARMER'S WIFE. An' now they're buildin' the wall again, count a
the govermin's changed.

FARMER. So the soldier boys turned us out on our land. Now
everyone's off to the work camp to work on the wall. We'd best
move sharp, do there'll be no more room.

FARMER'S WIFE. The women as well.

FARMER. An' the boy's off to be a soldier.

FARMER'S WIFE. We can't bait en an' dress en n' more.

LEAR. But they'll kill him in the army.

FARMER'S WIFE. We must hope they won't.

SON. Thass late. T'ent time t' natter. Doo come.

The SON *goes out.*

FARMER'S WIFE. We're speedin', boy.

The FARMER *and his* WIFE *go out after their* SON.

LEAR. I could learn to endure my blindness with patience, I could never endure this! (*Calls.*) Children! Ah!

LEAR *falls down on to his knees.*

FARMER'S WIFE (*off*). The poor gentleman's toppled over.

The FARMER *and his* WIFE *and* SON *hurry on.*

LEAR. I am the King! I kneel by this wall. How many lives have I ended here? Go away. Go anywhere. Go far away. Run. I will not move till you go!

FARMER'S WIFE. Do stand, sir.

LEAR. I've heard your voices. I'd never seen a poor man! You take too much pity out of me, if there's no pity I shall die of this grief.

SON. That ol' boy's a great rambler.

LEAR. They feed you and clothe you – is that why you can't see? All life seeks its safety. A wolf, a fox, a horse – they'd run away, they're sane. Why d'you run to meet your butchers? Why?

SON. I'll see you in the camp.

The FARMER'S SON *goes out.*

FARMER'S WIFE. Tent decent leavin' en out here on his own, dad.

FARMER. Poor man. If yoo take en someplace they'll beat en an' chain en. Let en be, he's at home in the fields. Let en bear his cross in peace.

The FARMER *and the* FARMER'S WIFE *go out.*

LEAR (*stumbles to his feet*). Men destroy themselves and say it's their duty? It's not possible! How can they be so abused? Cordelia doesn't know what she's doing! I must tell her – write to her!

GHOST. No, no, no! They never listen!

LEAR. I can't be silent! O my eyes! This crying's opened my wounds! There's blood again! Quick, quick, help me! My eyes, my eyes! I must stop her before I die!

LEAR *stumbles out on the* GHOST's *arm.*

Act Three

SCENE ONE

The GRAVEDIGGER'S BOY'*s house.*
More dilapidated, but obviously lived in. The stage is empty for a moment. THOMAS *and* JOHN *come in.*

THOMAS (*calls*). We're home! (*Stretches and yawns happily.*) I'm all in.

> JOHN *draws water from the well and washes himself.* SUSAN *comes to the door with* LEAR. THOMAS *embraces her.*

SUSAN. Have you been busy?
LEAR. No news from the village?
THOMAS. No.
LEAR. None? (THOMAS *starts to lead* LEAR *to a bench.*) Cordelia should have answered my last letter. It was stronger than the others. I thought she'd have to answer –
THOMAS (*calming him*). I know, I know.
JOHN. I'll eat in the village tonight with my girl's family.
SUSAN (*slightly annoyed*). You should have told me. (*To* THOMAS.) It won't be long.
THOMAS. I'm starving!

> SUSAN *goes into the house with* THOMAS. JOHN *throws his water away. A* SMALL MAN *comes in. He is dirty and frightened and in rags.*

SMALL MAN. I was lookin' – for someone. Could you give us some water?

> JOHN *nods to a pitcher by the well. The* SMALL MAN *drinks noisily.*

JOHN. You're off the road.

SMALL MAN (*sees* LEAR). Ah, sir. It was you I was lookin' for, sir. They said – (*He stops.*) You knew me when I was a soldier, sir. Small dark man. Black hair.

LEAR. What's your name?

SMALL MAN. O yes. McFearson.

JOHN. How did you get in that state?

THOMAS *comes out of the house. He puts his hand on* LEAR's *shoulder.*

SMALL MAN. On the road. Thass why I'm 'ungry.

LEAR. Yes, I think I remember you. If you're hungry you'd better stay to dinner.

SMALL MAN. Thank you, thanks.

LEAR. Give him John's. He's going down to the village. Take him into the house.

THOMAS *takes the* SMALL MAN *into the house.* THOMAS *turns in the doorway.*

THOMAS (*to* LEAR). He can't stay. Apart from anything else there isn't enough food.

LEAR. I'll tell him.

THOMAS *goes on into the house. The* GHOST *has come on. He looks thinner and more wasted.*

GHOST. D'you know who he is?

LEAR. A soldier.

JOHN *turns to watch* LEAR.

GHOST. That's right, a deserter. I suppose the fool didn't keep out of sight, moved by day, asked everyone where you were. It won't take them long to follow him. Get rid of the lot of them! Then we'll be safe.

The SMALL MAN *comes out of the house.*

SMALL MAN. Didn't want to get under the lady's feet. It's good of

you to let me – (*He stops.*) I thought, for old time's sake . . . The
'ole regiment said you was one a the best.

JOHN (*putting on his jacket*). I'm off.

> JOHN *goes and the* SMALL MAN *immediately sits down on the
> bench.*

SMALL MAN. Good old days, really. (*Laughs.*) Only yer never
know it at the time. Nice 'ere, nice place. You're very well fixed
– considerin'.

LEAR. Yes.

SMALL MAN. Mind you, yer must be hard pressed. Not a lot t' do
everythin'. Juss the two men an' the girl, is it? (*No reply.*) An'
you must take a fair bit a lookin' after. An' why shouldn't yer be
looked after? Yer deserve it. Yes. I was a batman – as I suppose
yer remember.

LEAR. I'm sorry. I was thinking about something else. I've written
to Cordelia, but she doesn't answer. Yes, there's just the four of
us. They moved in when the house was empty, and they've
looked after me since I came back. I thought I'd die but they
saved me. But tell me about your life. I'd like to know how
you've lived and what you've done.

SMALL MAN. O nothin'. Not t' interest your class a person. Not
worth tellin'.

LEAR. But you've fought in great wars and helped to make great
changes in the world.

SMALL MAN. What?

> THOMAS *comes out of the house and the* SMALL MAN *jumps up.*

O – this your place?

THOMAS. Where've you come from?

SMALL MAN. Well, my wife dies so I was on me own. I says t'
meself – travel! See the world while it's still there. New bed
every night, a new life every mornin' –

THOMAS. But why are you in that state?

SMALL MAN. Well. (*Sits.*) Yes, why shouldn't I tell yer. I wasn't goin' t' tell yer – the truth upsets people. But you're men of the world. I got beaten up. These thugs, they'd feed their own kids to a guard dog t' keep it quiet –

THOMAS. He's lying –

SMALL MAN. I take an oath – as I stand 'ere –

THOMAS. You're lying!

LEAR. Of course he's lying! Did it take you that long to find out?

THOMAS. Anyone could have sent him! He might be dangerous!

SMALL MAN. No, no, that's not true. Dangerous! (*Half laughs.*) God knows I couldn't 'urt a fly.

THOMAS. Then who are you? Tell me!

SMALL MAN. No! I came t' see 'im, not you!

THOMAS. Who are you?

SMALL MAN. Nobody! I'm from the wall a course – are you stupid? I ran away! I couldn't work. Anyone can see I'm sick. I spit blood. So they put me in a punishment squad. And then the black market . . . (*He stops.*) But if yer can't work they don't feed yer! So I ran. God knows what I was doin'. I must a bin off me 'ead. It's too late now.

THOMAS. But why did you come here?

SMALL MAN. I 'id in the trees but they was everywhere. – What made me what? They're all afraid in the camps so news travels fast. Thass 'ow we 'eard a you.

SUSAN (*off*). It's ready.

SMALL MAN. When I come here I said – say it ain't true, juss talk, an' they give yer up? O Chriss, I didn't know what t' think. Thass why I said yer knew me. You bein' blind I thought –

LEAR. What did you hear in the camp?

SMALL MAN. Yer wan'a get rid a the army an' blow up the wall, an' shut the camps an' send the prisoners home. Yer give money to a deserter.

THOMAS. Did you?

SMALL MAN. An' I was goin t' die on the wall.

JOHN *comes in.*

JOHN. There's soldiers coming up the hill.

LEAR. Take him in the woods.

THOMAS. Lear! –

LEAR. No! Tell me all that later. Hide him. Warn Susan. He hasn't been here.

> SMALL MAN *whimpers*. THOMAS *hurries with him into the house.*

Sit down. (JOHN *and* LEAR *sit. Pause. He talks to fill the silence.*) Your young girl will be waiting in the village.

JOHN. Yes. I'm late again. Something always happens, and she gets upset . . .

LEAR. Will you marry her?

JOHN (*listening*). They're coming.

LEAR. Have you asked her? She might not have you.

JOHN. No, not yet.

> *An* OFFICER *and* THREE SOLDIERS (P, Q, *and* R) *come in.*

There's some soldiers here, Lear.

LEAR (*nods*). Is there anything you want? Water or food?

OFFICER. Who else is here?

LEAR. There's a woman in the house and another man somewhere.

OFFICER. Who else?

LEAR. No one.

OFFICER (*to* SOLDIERS). Look round. (SOLDIERS P *and* Q *go into the house. To* JOHN.) Have you seen anyone?

LEAR. He was at work, he's just got back.

SOLDIER R (*offering to go*). Scout round the woods, sir?

OFFICER (*irritated*). You'll never find him in there.

> SUSAN *comes out of the house and stands still.*

(*To* LEAR.) A man was asking for you in the village. Small, dark man.

LEAR. Well, he'll turn up if they told him where I am. I'll let you know.

SOLDIERS P *and* Q *come out of the house.*

SOLDIER P (*shakes his head*). Dead.

OFFICER (*to* LEAR). Very well. This place will be watched in future.

The OFFICER *and* THREE SOLDIERS *leave.*

JOHN. They've gone.

LEAR. Go and see them off.

JOHN *goes out.* SUSAN *goes upstage and calls.*

SUSAN. Tom! (*To* LEAR.) They can't do anything to us. We didn't ask him to come. I'll give him some food to take with him. If he's caught he can say he stole it.

THOMAS *comes in.* SUSAN *goes to him.*

THOMAS. What happened? What did they say?

LEAR. I don't know. I didn't listen. They were just soldiers. No rank.

THOMAS. We must get rid of him quick. If he's caught here now we're for it.

BEN, *the young orderly, comes in. He is dirty, dishevelled, ragged and breathless. They stare at him.*

BEN. There were soldiers out on the road. I 'ad t' crawl the last bit on me 'ands an' knees.

The SMALL MAN *comes in and watches.*

(*Goes to* LEAR.) I looked after you in the cage, sir. They put me on the wall for floggin' snout t' cons.

LEAR. Yes. You fed me in prison. You can stay here.

THOMAS. No!

LEAR. He can stay.

THOMAS. But we'll all be responsible. They'll say we encourage them! They'll blame us for everything! It's insane!

LEAR. Where else can he go? *You* go if you're afraid!

THOMAS. How can you be so obstinate, how can you be such a fool?

BEN (*to* LEAR). Yeh, you ain' some prisoner no one's ever 'eard of, they can't mess you about.

LEAR. No, you mustn't say that. I'm not a king. I have no power. But you can stay. You're doing no harm. Now I'm hungry, take me inside. I'll write to Cordelia again. She means well, she only needs someone to make her see sense. Take me in. I came here when I was cold and hungry and afraid. I wasn't turned away, and I won't turn anyone away. They can eat my food while it lasts and when it's gone they can go if they like, but I won't send anyone away. That's how I'll end my life. I'll be shut up in a grave soon, and till then this door is open. (*He smiles.*)

> LEAR *and the others go towards the house.*

SMALL MAN (*following them. He speaks half to himself*). Thass all very well. But yer never seen 'is sort on the wall. We can't let everyone in. We 'ave t' act fly.

> *The* SMALL MAN *follows the others into the house.*

SCENE TWO

Same.
Months later. Many strangers have gathered to listen to LEAR.
THOMAS *leads him out of the house and down to the audience and turns* LEAR *to face them. As* LEAR *comes down a few* STRANGERS *say 'Good morning' and* LEAR *smiles at them and says 'Good morning'.*
THOMAS *stands at* LEAR'S *side and* JOHN *stands a little way back. The* STRANGERS *watch with respect.*

LEAR (*to the audience*). A man woke up one morning and found he'd lost his voice. So he went to look for it, and when he came to the wood there was the bird who'd stolen it. It was singing beautifully and the man said 'Now I sing so beautifully I shall be rich and famous'. He put the bird in a cage and said 'When I open my mouth wide you must sing'. Then he went to the king and said 'I will sing your majesty's praises'. But when he opened his mouth the bird could only groan and cry because it was in a cage, and the king had the man whipped. The man took the bird home, but his family couldn't stand the bird's groaning and crying and they left him. So in the end the man took the bird back to the wood and let it out of the cage. But the man believed the king had treated him unjustly and he kept saying to himself 'The king's a fool' and as the bird still had the man's voice it kept singing this all over the wood and soon the other birds learned it. The next time the king went hunting he was surprised to hear all the birds singing 'The king's a fool'. He caught the bird who'd started it and pulled out its feathers, broke its wings and nailed it to a branch as a warning to all the other birds. The forest was silent. And just as the bird had the man's voice the man now had the bird's pain. He ran round silently waving his head and stamping his feet, and he was locked up for the rest of his life in a cage.

The STRANGERS *murmur.*

A STRANGER. Tell me, Lear –
THOMAS. Later. He must rest now.

> THOMAS *leads* LEAR *to one side. The* STRANGERS *break up into groups and talk. A few leave.*

I want you to send Ben back to the wall.
LEAR. Why?
THOMAS. Hundreds of people come to hear you now. The government can't let this go on, and they could crush us like that! We need support. We must infiltrate the camps.

> BEN *has been watching intensely. He comes over to them.*

BEN. Has he told you? I'll give myself up. They'll put me in a punishment squad. I'll be beaten and starved and worked like an animal. I may not survive – but at least I'll use what time I've got left. I'll help them to organize and be ready. I can bring them hope. You must give me a message to take –

LEAR. If I saw Christ on his cross I would spit at him.

BEN. What?

LEAR. Take me away.

THOMAS. You haven't listened!

BEN. Listen to us!

LEAR. Take me away!

> THOMAS *leads* LEAR *towards the house. Some of the* STRANGERS *meet him and take him inside.* BEN *and* THOMAS *look at one another in silence.* SUSAN *puts an arm round* THOMAS *to comfort him.*

THOMAS. You look tired.

SUSAN. No.

THOMAS (*sitting down with her*). Don't work too hard.

SUSAN. I'm not.

THOMAS (*presses her*). And don't run round after all these people. They can look after themselves.

SUSAN. O I don't mind them. But when we have our baby –

THOMAS. You don't have to worry about that. They'll all help.

SUSAN. Only it's a small house. Sometimes I'd like to speak to you and there are so many people –

THOMAS. Speak about what? You can always speak to me.

SUSAN. O I don't know. I meant . . . (*She is silent.*)

THOMAS (*thinking about* LEAR. *After a slight pause*). We talk to people but we don't really help them. We shouldn't let them come here if that's all we can do. It's dangerous to tell the truth, truth without power is always dangerous. And we *should* fight! Freedom's not an idea, it's a passion! If you haven't got it you fight like a fish out of water fighting for air!

> *The* STRANGERS *who left hurry on quickly.*

STRANGERS (*quietly and intensely*). Soldiers. Soldiers.

> THOMAS *stands*.

THOMAS. What is it?

> *The* OLD COUNCILLOR, *an* OFFICER *and* SOLDIERS P, Q *and* R *come on*.

OFFICER (*reads from a form*). Rossman – (BEN *comes forward*.) – and – (*He points at the* SMALL MAN *as he tries to slip away*.) – grab him – (SOLDIERS P *and* Q *stop the* SMALL MAN.) – Jones –

SMALL MAN. Thass not me! I'm Simpson!

OFFICER. – I'm taking you into custody as absentees from your work camps.

> LEAR *is led from the house. He stands on the steps surrounded by* STRANGERS.

LEAR. Who is it? What d'you want?

OFFICER. You're harbouring deserters.

LEAR. I don't ask my friends who they are.

BEN. Let them take me!

SOLDIER R. Shut it!

OFFICER. I'm returning them under guard to the area military commandant.

SMALL MAN (*tries to go to* LEAR *but the* SOLDIERS *stop him*). For God's sake what d'you want me for? Yer can see I'm ill! What work can I do? I'm in everyone's way. For God's sake leave me alone.

OFFICER. You're not going back to work. Certain economic offences have been made capital with retrospective effect. You were found guilty of dealing on the unauthorized market. The revised sentence is mandatory.

SMALL MAN (*bewildered*). I don't understand that.

OFFICER. You're a social liability. You're going back to be hanged.

SMALL MAN (*vaguely*). Yer can't . . . I've already been dealt with. It's on me records, sir. I don't understand.

LEAR. Take me to him. (LEAR *is led to the* OFFICER. *He puts his hand on the* OFFICER's *arm. Quietly.*) You're a soldier, how many deaths are on your conscience? Don't burden yourself with two more. Go back and say you can't find them.

COUNCILLOR. Lear, every word you say is treason.

LEAR. Who's that? Who's there?

COUNCILLOR. I was your minister –

LEAR. Yes – I know you!

COUNCILLOR. Out of respect for your age and sufferings Cordelia has tolerated your activities, but now they must stop. In future you will not speak in public or involve yourself in any public affairs. Your visitors will be vetted by the area military authorities. All these people must go. The government will appoint a man and woman to look after you. You will live in decent quietness, as a man of your years should.

LEAR. Are you in their new government?

COUNCILLOR. Like many of my colleagues I gave the new undertaking of loyalty. I've always tried to serve people. I see that as my chief duty. If we abandon the administration there'd be chaos.

LEAR. Yes, yes – but you won't hang this man for money?

SMALL MAN. The records must be wrong . . . That's it!

OFFICER. Take him down to the road.

SMALL MAN (*bewildered. Whimpers*). No.

LEAR (*to* COUNCILLOR). Stop them.

COUNCILLOR. It isn't my concern at all. I came to speak to *you*.

LEAR. I see. Savages have taken my power. You commit crimes and call them the law! The giant must stand on his toes to prove he's tall! – No, I'm wrong to shout at you, you have so much to do, things to put right, all my mistakes, I understand all that . . . But he's a little swindler! A petty swindler! Think of the crimes you commit every day in your office, day after day till it's just routine, think of the waste and misery of that!

COUNCILLOR. I was sent to talk to you as an old friend, not to be insulted, Lear. He'll be taken back to the wall and

hanged. And – as you are interested in my views – I think he
should be.

LEAR. O I know what you think! Whatever's trite and vulgar and
hard and shallow and cruel, with no mercy or sympathy – that's
what you think, and you're proud of it! You good, decent,
honest, upright, lawful men who believe in order – when the last
man dies, you will have killed him! I have lived with murderers
and thugs, there are limits to their greed and violence, but you
decent, honest men devour the earth!

SOLDIERS P *and* Q *start to take the* SMALL MAN *out.*

SMALL MAN. No – stop them!

LEAR. There's nothing I can do! The government's mad. The
law's mad.

SMALL MAN (*throws himself at* LEAR). Then why did yer let me
come 'ere? O God, I know I'm bad sometimes and I don't
deserve to – O God, please!

LEAR. There's nothing I can do!

SMALL MAN. Then I should a stayed an' be shot like a dog. I lived
like a dog, what did it matter? It'd be finished now. Why've I
suffered all this?

The SMALL MAN *is taken out crying. The* OFFICER, OLD
COUNCILLOR, BEN *and* SOLDIERS *go with him.* LEAR *starts
to push the* STRANGERS *out.*

LEAR. Send them away!

JOHN. You'll fall!

LEAR (*stumbling up and down. Flailing with his stick*). Send them
away! The government's given its orders. Power has spoken.
Get out! What are you doing here? What have I been telling
you? There's nothing to learn here! I'm a fool! A fool! Get out!

SUSAN (*turning away*). O God.

LEAR. Send them away! Throw them out!

THOMAS. They're going. (*He talks as quietly as he can to the*
STRANGERS.) Wait in the village. I'll talk to him.

LEAR. Get out! Get out! I said get rid of them!

> *The* STRANGERS *go.* LEAR, SUSAN, THOMAS *and* JOHN *are left.*

THOMAS. They've gone.

LEAR. Get out! All of you! Leave me alone!

THOMAS. No! I must know what to tell them. We're not backing out now.

LEAR. O go away! Go! Go! Go! Who is this stupid man who keeps talking to me?

JOHN (*pulls* THOMAS). Come on.

THOMAS. Sit! I'll go if you sit!

LEAR. O go . . . Go.

> LEAR *sits.* THOMAS, JOHN *and* SUSAN *go into the house.*

What can I do? I left my prison, pulled it down, broke the key, and still I'm a prisoner. I hit my head against a wall all the time. There's a wall everywhere. I'm buried alive in a wall. Does this suffering and misery last for ever? Do we work to build ruins, waste all these lives to make a desert no one could live in? There's no one to explain it to me, no one I can go to for justice. I'm old, I should know how to live by now, but I know nothing, I can do nothing, I am nothing.

> *The* GHOST *comes in. It is thinner, shrunk, a livid white.*

GHOST. Look at my hands! They're like claws. See how thin I am.

LEAR. Yes, you. Go with the rest. Get out. It's finished. There's nothing here now, nothing. Nothing's left.

GHOST. There's too much. Send these people away. Let them learn to bear their own sufferings. No, that hurts too much. That's what you can't bear: they suffer and no one can give them justice.

LEAR. Every night my life is laid waste by a cry. I go out in the dark but I never find who's there. How do most men live? They're hungry and no one feeds them, so they call for help and

no one comes. And when their hunger's worse they scream –
and jackals and wolves come to tear them to pieces.

GHOST. Yes. That's the world you have to learn to live in. Learn
it! Let me poison the well.

LEAR. Why?

GHOST. Then no one can live here, they'll have to leave you alone.
There's a spring hidden in the wood. I'll take you there every
day to drink. Lie down. Look how tired you are. Lie down.

LEAR lies down.

Cordelia will come tomorrow and you can tell her you know
how to keep silent at last.

*It's dark. LEAR sleeps on the bench. JOHN comes out of the
house with a bundle. He crosses the stage. SUSAN comes to the
door. He sees her and stops.*

SUSAN. Why are you taking your things?

JOHN. Come with me.

SUSAN. No.

JOHN. I love you. Your husband doesn't any more. He's full of
Lear.

SUSAN (*angrily*). He does love me!

JOHN. I see. (*Slight pause.*) I was used to saying nothing, but you
came out so I told you. How beautiful you are. There's nothing
to say, you know all about me. I'll wait in the village. If you
don't come I'll marry the girl down there. But I'll wait a few
days, or I'll always be sorry.

*JOHN goes. SUSAN sits on the steps and starts to cry, quietly and
methodically. THOMAS comes in the doorway behind her.*

THOMAS. Stop crying.

SUSAN. Take me away.

THOMAS. I can't leave him now. It'd be cruel.

SUSAN (*still crying*). I know he's mad. You shouldn't keep me
here when I'm like this.

THOMAS (*calmly and quietly*). There's been enough tears for one day. Stop crying and come inside.

> THOMAS *goes back into the house.* SUSAN *stops crying and follows him in.*

SCENE THREE

Woods.
LEAR *is alone. He wears outdoor clothes. He gropes on his hands and knees. Off, the pigs start to squeal angrily.* LEAR *stands. The* GHOST *comes in. Its flesh has dried up, its hair is matted, its face is like a seashell, the eyes are full of terror.*

GHOST. I frighten the pigs. They run when they see me.

LEAR. I was collecting acorns for them. (*He stands.*)

GHOST. The soldiers are moving into the village. They're sealing you off. Will you send the people away?

LEAR. No.

GHOST. I thought you'd forget all this: crowds, wars, arguments. . . . We could have been happy living here. I used to be happy. I'd have led you about and watched you grow old, your beautiful old age . . .

LEAR. We buried your body here. And Warrington's. It's beautiful under the trees. I thought I might think of something to tell Cordelia out here. I don't know . . . They're coming to bury me and I'm still asking how to live. Can you hear the wind?

GHOST. No. My mind goes. You hear very well when you're blind.

LEAR. Yes.

GHOST. Can you hear an owl on the hill?

LEAR. Yes.

GHOST. But not the fox.

LEAR. No.

GHOST. No. (*He starts to cry.*)

LEAR (*listens to him crying*). Why?

GHOST. Because I'm dead. I knew how to live. You'll never know. It was so easy, I had everything I wanted here. I was afraid sometimes, like sheep are, but it never haunted me, it would go . . . Now I'm dead I'm afraid of death. I'm wasting away, my mind doesn't work . . . I go away somewhere and suddenly I find myself standing by the house or out in the fields . . . It happens more now . . .

> CORDELIA *and the* CARPENTER *come in.*

CORDELIA. Lear. (*She holds* LEAR's *hand for a moment.*) I've brought my husband.

LEAR. You've been to the house? Did it upset you?

CORDELIA. No. I wanted to see it.

LEAR. Are you well?

CORDELIA. Yes. And you? D'you need anything?

LEAR. No.

CORDELIA. I came because the cabinet wants you to be tried. There could only be one sentence. Your daughters were killed. And it's clear there's no real difference between you and them.

LEAR. None.

CORDELIA. You were here when they killed my husband. I watched them kill him. I covered my face with my hands, but my fingers opened so I watched. I watched them rape me, and John kill them, and my child miscarry. I didn't miss anything. I watched and I said we won't be at the mercy of brutes any-more, we'll live a new life and help one another. The govern-ment's creating that new life – you must stop speaking against us.

LEAR. Stop people listening.

CORDELIA. I can't. You say what they want to hear.

LEAR. If that's true – if only some of them want to hear – I must speak.

CORDELIA. Yes, you sound like the voice of my conscience. But if you listened to everything your conscience told you you'd go mad. You'd never get anything done – and there's a lot to do, some of it very hard.

GHOST. Tell her I'm here. Make her talk about me.

LEAR. Don't build the wall.

CORDELIA. We must.

LEAR. Then nothing's changed! A revolution must at least reform!

CORDELIA. Everything *else* is changed!

LEAR. Not if you keep the wall! Pull it down!

CORDELIA. We'd be attacked by our enemies!

LEAR. The wall will destroy you. It's already doing it. How can I make you see?

GHOST. Tell her I'm here. Tell her.

CARPENTER. We came to talk to you, not listen. My wife wants to tell you something.

LEAR. She came like the rest! And she'll listen like the rest! I didn't go out of my way to make trouble. But I will not be quiet when people come here. And if you stop them – that would be easy! – they'll know I'm here or was here *once*! I've suffered so much, I made all the mistakes in the world and I pay for each of them. I cannot be forgotten. I am in their minds. To kill me you must kill them all. Yes, that's who I am. Listen, Cordelia. You have two enemies, lies *and* the truth. You sacrifice truth to destroy lies, and you sacrifice life to destroy death. It isn't sane. You squeeze a stone till your hand bleeds and call that a miracle. I'm old, but I'm as weak and clumsy as a child, too heavy for my legs. But I've learned this, and you must learn it or you'll die. Listen, Cordelia. If a God had made the world, might would always be right, that would be so wise, we'd be spared so much suffering. But we made the world – out of our smallness and weakness. Our lives are awkward and fragile and we have only one thing to keep us sane: pity, and the man without pity is mad.

The GHOST *starts to cry as* CORDELIA *speaks.*

CORDELIA. You only understand self-pity. We must go back, the government's waiting. There are things you haven't been told. We have other opponents, more ruthless than you. In this situation a good government acts strongly. I knew you wouldn't co-operate, but I wanted to come and tell you this before we put you on trial: we'll make the society you only dream of.

LEAR. It's strange that you should have me killed, Cordelia, but it's obvious you would. How simple! Your Law always does more harm than crime, and your morality is a form of violence.

CORDELIA (*to* CARPENTER). The sooner it's finished now the better. Call a cabinet for the morning.

CORDELIA *and the* CARPENTER *go out.*

GHOST. Why didn't you tell her I was here? She wanted to talk about me. She couldn't forget me. I made love to her in that house night after night, and on this grass. Look at me now! I've turned into *this* – I can't even touch her!

LEAR. Where are you going?

GHOST. I can watch her go.

The GHOST *goes out.* THOMAS *and* SUSAN *come on. They have dressed up a little because of the visitors.*

THOMAS. We waited till they went. Shall I take you back?

LEAR. Listen, I must talk to you. I'm going on a journey and Susan will lead me.

THOMAS. Yes, go into hiding! Don't let them get their filthy hands on you.

LEAR. Tomorrow morning we'll get up and have breakfast together and you'll go to work, but Susan will stay with me. She may not be back tomorrow evening, but she'll be back soon, I promise you. You're fond of me and I've been happy with you. I'm lucky. Now I have only one more wish – to live till I'm much older and become as cunning as the fox, who knows how to live. *Then* I could teach you.

Off, distant squealing of angry pigs, further off than at the end of Act One, Scene Seven.

THOMAS. The pigs!
SUSAN. What is it?

SUSAN *and* THOMAS *run off.* LEAR *stands by himself.*

THOMAS (*off*). They've gone mad!
SUSAN (*off*). Quick!
THOMAS (*off*). That way!
SUSAN (*off*). Look out!
THOMAS (*off*). Berserk! Wup-wup-wup-wup-wup-wup-wup!
SUSAN (*off*). Wup-wup-wup! Mad!

The GHOST *stumbles in. It is covered with blood. The pig squeals slowly die out. A few more isolated calls of 'wup'.*

GHOST. The pigs! I'm torn! They gored me! Help me, help me! I'll die!
LEAR (*holds him*). I can't!
GHOST. Lear! Hold me!
LEAR. No, too late! It's far too late! You were killed long ago! You must die! I love you, I'll always remember you, but I can't help you. Die, for your own sake die!
GHOST. O Lear, I am dead!

The GHOST's *head falls back. It is dead. It drops at* LEAR's *feet. The calls and pig squeals stop.*

LEAR. I see my life, a black tree by a pool. The branches are covered with tears. The tears are shining with light. The wind blows the tears in the sky. And my tears fall down on me.

SCENE FOUR

The wall.
A steep earth bank. A stack of tools at the bottom of the bank. Clear
daylight. SUSAN *leads* LEAR *on. He has no stick.*

SUSAN. This is the wall.
LEAR. Where are the tools?
SUSAN. On the ground in front of you.
LEAR. You were angry with me.
SUSAN. I was, but I'm not now.
LEAR (*kisses her*). Goodbye. Go back alone.
SUSAN. I can't! Who'll look after you. My husband would be
angry.
LEAR. No. He'll understand now.

> SUSAN *goes out.* LEAR *goes to the tools. He finds a shovel.*

A shovel. (*He climbs the wall.*) It's built to last. So steep, and my
breath's short. (*He reaches the top.*) The wind's cold, I must be
quick. (*He digs the shovel in.*) Work soon warms you up.

> *He throws a shovel of earth down the side and digs the shovel in*
> *again. A* BOY *comes on and stares at* LEAR. LEAR *throws*
> *another shovel of earth down. The* BOY *goes out in the direction*
> *he came.*

This will be three. (*He digs the shovel in again.*) The tool's got
no edge. No one cares for it.

> *A group of* WORKERS *come on and stare at* LEAR. *He leaves the*
> *shovel stuck in the earth. He takes off his coat and folds it neatly.*
> *A junior officer comes in. It is the* FARMER'S SON. *He watches.*
> LEAR *lays his folded coat on the ground and turns back to the*
> *shovel.*

FARMER'S SON. Oi, I know yoo, boy. What yoo up to now?
LEAR (*he grips the shovel*). I'm not as fit as I was.

He digs up a shovel of earth. The FARMER'S SON *aims his pistol.*

But I can still make my mark.

LEAR *throws the earth down the side. The* FARMER'S SON *fires.* LEAR *is winged. The shovel stands upright in the earth.* LEAR *spits on his hands and grips the shovel.*

One more.

He half-throws, half-scrapes more earth down. The FARMER'S SON *aims, fires, and hits.* LEAR *is killed instantly and falls down the wall. Some of the* WORKERS *move towards the body with curiosity.*

FARMER'S SON. Leave that. They'll pick en up. Off now.

The WORKERS *go quickly and orderly. One of them looks back. The* FARMER'S SON *shepherds them off, and marches off after them.* LEAR's *body is left alone on stage.*

END